UNSOLVED
MYSTERIES OF
WORLD WAR II

UNSOLVED MYSTERIES OF WORLD WAR II

FROM NAZI GHOST TRAINS AND TOKYO ROSE TO THE DAY LOS ANGELES WAS ATTACKED BY PHANTOM FIGHTERS

MICHAEL FITZGERALD

PICTURE CREDITS

All pictures are © Getty Images

This edition published in 2022 by Arcturus Publishing Limited
26/27 Bickels Yard, 151–153 Bermondsey Street,
London SE1 3HA

AD005921UK

Printed in the UK

MIX
Paper from
responsible sources
FSC® C171272

CONTENTS

INTRODUCTION

World War II is one of the best-documented eras in history. Over the course of time secret archives have been opened that have shed new light on previously doubtful events. DNA testing now makes it possible to positively identify uncertain remains and there are far fewer unknown facts about the conflict than in the 1980s.

In spite of our extensive knowledge of the period many aspects of it are still rather unclear. A large number of these mysteries remain enigmas while in other cases probable explanations are now available.

Unsolved Mysteries of World War II deals with a wide range of topics. Did a German woman pilot fly to New York and Michigan, for example, and why did two German submarines disappear for two months after the end of the war before finally surrendering – to Argentina?

Another incident, the 1939 bomb plot in a Munich beer cellar, has attracted a variety of conspiracy theories. *Unsolved Mysteries* unravels the story and separates fact from myth, propaganda and downright fabrication to suggest the most plausible explanation for the failed assassination attempt on Hitler.

Unsolved Mysteries examines stories from Britain, America, Russia, France, Germany, Italy, North Africa and Japan. While doing so, it considers several mysterious deaths and the possible survival of various people including Hitler and Bormann.

Espionage during the war involved considerable disinformation by both the Allied and the Axis powers. The 'Velser Affair', where a number of Dutch Resistance fighters were murdered in the closing stages of the war, remains a baffling mystery. Whether they were killed by Nazis, collaborators or Dutch anti-Communists is still unclear. Police officers who attempted to investigate the murders received death threats.

The Battle of Los Angeles involved considerable military activity against what were believed to be Japanese aircraft. The theory that Los Angeles was under attack by enemy aircraft has long been disproved but the true nature of the events remains uncertain.

World War II saw looting on an epic scale and the whereabouts of many of these 'lost treasures' is still unknown. For instance, the famous 'Amber Room' presented to Peter the Great by the King of Prussia vanished at the end of the war. Was it destroyed by bombing and shelling, stolen by the Nazis or removed by the Russians? The whereabouts of the Nazi 'blood flag' and Hitler's globe – immortalized by Charlie Chaplin in the film *The Great Dictator* – also remain unknown. Nazi gold reserves held by the Reichsbank were plundered too, by different people and groups including the SS, the Red Army and the US military. Their present location is still an enigma.

The World Trade Fair in 1940 saw a mysterious explosion which killed two policemen. Responsibility for planting the bomb has never been satisfactorily established.

Military mysteries include the unexpected collapse of the French Army in 1940, the failure of German tanks to advance against Dunkirk and the lack of adequate protection for and communication with the US Pacific Fleet at Pearl Harbor.

Unsolved Mysteries of World War II deals with these and many other secrets of the war. Hess's flight to Britain and the actor Leslie

*Hitler at the Bürgerbraükeller, Munich in 1938. In the background is the **Blutfahne** ('blood flag') held by its special attendant Jakob Grimminger. The flag disappeared in 1944 and was never seen again.*

Howard's death in a civilian plane shot down by the Luftwaffe are well known. Other stories in *Unsolved Mysteries* are less familiar.

While dealing with many incidents of major importance *Unsolved Mysteries* also examines more 'minor' events during the war. There are still questions about many aspects of World War II that remain unanswered. In some cases probable explanations exist but other secrets have never been revealed. The truth about them may never be known.

CHAPTER ONE
THE BATTLE OF LOS ANGELES

CHAPTER ONE

The Battle of Los Angeles was a curious event that took place between 24 and 25 February 1942. Explanations for it vary wildly. It occurred less than three months after the Japanese attack on Pearl Harbor and only a day after Japanese submarine 1-17 bombarded Ellwood. The first thought was that an air raid had been launched from Japan but this idea was quickly dismissed by the Secretary of the Navy.

The night of 24–25 February saw a flurry of air raid sirens. Air raid wardens rushed into position and a total blackout of the area was ordered. Then at 3.16 a.m. the 37th Coast Artillery Brigade took the decision to begin firing .50 calibre machine guns and 12.8-pound anti-aircraft shells at the unidentified object. Pilots were also alerted but no planes were sent up into the air. The firing continued until 4.14 a.m., when the all-clear signal was sounded, and the blackout was lifted by 7.21 a.m.

The shells damaged buildings and vehicles and five people lost their lives – two as a result of heart attacks induced by the stress of the hostilities and three in car accidents. Within a few hours of the raid being terminated, the Navy Secretary held a press briefing in which he attributed the incident to what he called 'war nerves'. General George C. Marshall suggested that commercial planes might have been used as a psychological warfare tactic.

The press remained suspicious. There was speculation that the unprepared US authorities had been caught out by secret Japanese attacks and were trying to conceal their own inefficiency. Ideas about hidden bases in Mexico and a fleet of Japanese submarines offshore armed with long-range weapons were put forward. Another theory was that the government had staged the whole thing deliberately to give it an excuse to move industries situated on the coast to sites further inland.

Santa Monica Congressman Leland Ford demanded a full Congressional investigation, declaring:

> *None of the explanations so far offered removed the episode from the category of 'complete mystification' ... this was either a practice raid, or a raid to throw a scare into 2,000,000 people, or a mistaken identity raid, or a raid to lay a political foundation to take away Southern California's war industries.*

His demands were ignored and the events remained a mystery and the subject of speculation and conspiracy theories.

The North American Aviation factory at Inglewood, near LA, ramped up its production of P-51 Mustangs ready to rebuff marauding enemy aircraft, 1942.

ELLWOOD ATTACK

Pearl Harbor was still fresh in people's minds and the submarine attack on Ellwood the day before had created a sense of panic. In this atmosphere, it is not surprising that the event became a major news story and that conspiracy theories were soon woven around it.

The devastation caused by the raid on Pearl Harbor was magnified by Japanese naval activity and Japan sent seven submarines to patrol the West Coast of America. Twice, the submarines became involved in fights with American naval or air forces and they sank several merchant ships. By late December, they returned to Japan for maintenance and supplies.

Japanese submarine *1–17* then returned to American waters. Before the war its commander, Kozo Nishino, had been in charge of a merchant ship and had refilled his vessel with oil before returning to Japan. While walking to the refinery he tripped and fell into some prickly pear cactus. The oil workers laughed when he had cactus spines removed from his buttocks and there was speculation that this incident may have led Nishino to target the oil refinery when his submarine was within range of it.

Nishino ordered his gun crew to aim at an aviation fuel tank and their initial gunfire landed close to the storage tanks. The few oil workers on duty at first thought the noise was due to an internal explosion. Then one of them saw the submarine. When the second tank was targeted the refinery staff called the police, but several rounds had been fired by the time that decision was taken.

More shells hit a nearby ranch, while another passed over Wheeler's Inn, and the Santa Barbara County Sheriff's Office was alerted. Another shell struck and damaged the Ellwood Pier. The firing destroyed a derrick and a pump house and damaged a catwalk. The whole operation lasted for 20 minutes before

Nishino gave the order to his crew to cease firing. Thirteen shells in all were fired.

As soon as news of the attack spread, planes were sent to the area to pursue the raider. Three more bombers joined the attempt to destroy the submarine but none were able to hit their target. Air Force commanders only deployed these small quantities of aircraft because they feared that the raid was a diversionary one to decoy their resources away from the real target. Japanese-Americans who were loyal to the United States immediately warned that the very next day might see an aerial assault on Los Angeles.

'AERIAL BATTLE'

The Ellwood attack created panic out of all proportion to its effectiveness. With the memory of the raid fresh in people's minds, the following day saw a sustained 'aerial battle' against an unknown and still unidentified 'intruder'.

Following the Ellwood raid naval intelligence warned of an attack within the next ten hours or so. That evening there were many reports of flares and flashing lights in the region of defence plants. Eventually the various 'alerts' were cancelled but on the morning of 25 February 'hostilities' commenced in earnest.

They began with radar operators picking up a target 120 miles (193 km) to the west of Los Angeles. Air Force planes remained on the ground, but anti-aircraft batteries were put into a state of readiness. Radar tracking soon pointed to a target that was only a few miles off the coast and at 2.21 a.m. a blackout was ordered. Widespread reports of sightings of 'enemy planes' soon followed.

All trace of the target then vanished from the radar. However, witnesses reported seeing planes in the vicinity of Long Beach and a colonel in the coastal artillery reported seeing 'about 25 planes at 12,000 feet' over the city of Los Angeles. Around 20 minutes later a balloon with a red flare was observed over Santa Monica. It was promptly attacked by four anti-aircraft batteries. Following their assault on the balloon, 'the air over Los Angeles erupted like a volcano'.

At 3.16 a.m. Los Angeles heard the sound of air raid sirens. Anti-aircraft and machine guns began firing at targets from Santa Monica to Culver City. During this alert over 1,400 rounds were fired. Thousands of people saw the anti-aircraft batteries firing and there are many eyewitness accounts of the strange events of that early morning in February. They are, perhaps understandably, not consistent and often appear confused. There is very little agreement on the details of what was seen.

Some witnesses describe a craft that resembled a Zeppelin airship, while others insist that the object was more like a balloon. A number describe seeing aircraft. More baffling reports claim the object resembled a giant butterfly or a coffee pot.

In the confusion and panic it is understandable that witnesses gave different accounts of what they saw. It is perhaps more surprising that not only some anti-aircraft gunners but also various pilots describe the events differently.

Some observers describe seeing a single plane and others report seeing an entire squadron of Japanese aircraft or a fleet of airships that they insist were being chased by US fighters. Nobody suggested extraterrestrial invaders. That particular spin on the story came years later.

NEWSPAPER THEORIES

Following the bizarre 'battle', newspapers put forward a series of wild theories to account for the strange events. Some claimed that Japanese aircraft had flown right across Los Angeles and that the military were too embarrassed to admit that they had been caught out by the invaders. A popular conspiracy theory was that defence manufacturers had organized a phoney raid using civilian planes to frighten the government into allowing them to move their factories further inland.

The various government departments were unable to agree on either the details of what had taken place or an explanation for it. Frank Knox, Secretary of the Navy, announced at a press conference on 25 February that the raid had been a false alarm. He admitted that the West Coast of America was now vulnerable to enemy attack and suggested that any vital factories or other manufacturing facilities by the sea should be moved inland.

The army was very uncertain about the events of that night. Western Defence Command passed on a report to Washington shortly after the end of the raid which suggested that it was highly probable that no attack had taken place. They announced that 'most previous reports had been greatly exaggerated'. The Fourth Air Force also concluded that no aircraft of any kind had flown over Los Angeles that night.

Next day, following interviews with many eyewitnesses, the army decided that there had been between one and five unidentified planes flying over Los Angeles. This then became the official War Department explanation of the incident. Secretary for War Henry Stimson put forward two possible theories as to what the mysterious craft were. One was that they were light aircraft launched from Japanese submarines and the other was that they were commercial planes flown by the Japanese from concealed sites in California or Mexico. He believed that they were reconnaissance aircraft trying to locate anti-aircraft defence facilities in the area and had also been intended to demoralize civilian morale.

The media, unconvinced by the various official explanations and perplexed by the different 'solutions' offered, began to

CHAPTER ONE

make accusations of a cover-up. On 26 February, the *Los Angeles Times* carried a front-page editorial declaring that the official explanations made no sense. In view of 'the considerable public excitement and confusion' caused by the events, it said, a proper investigation was necessary and the public had a right to know the truth.

On 27 February the *Washington Post* described the authorities as having maintained what it called a 'stubborn silence' and as having panicked in the face of uncertain events. The newspaper dismissed the army's suggestion of commercial aircraft, declaring that it 'explains everything except where the planes came from, whither they were going, and why no American planes were sent in pursuit of them'.

The *New York Times* on 28 February found the whole affair utterly baffling. It stated:

> *If the batteries were firing on nothing at all, as Secretary Knox implies, it is a sign of expensive incompetence and jitters. If the batteries were firing on real planes, some of them as low as 9,000 feet, as Secretary Stimson declares, why were they completely ineffective? Why did no American planes go up to engage them, or even to identify them? What would have happened if this had been a real air raid?*

The reality was that American anti-aircraft defences were totally unprepared for any kind of air raid. Had the strange events of that night been a genuine Japanese attack, it would have caused widespread destruction.

At the end of the war, when they were specifically asked about the Los Angeles affair, the Japanese authorities said that none of their planes were in the area at the time. A few were launched from submarines operated off Seattle at a later date, but on the night in question not a single Japanese aircraft was anywhere near the zone.

As there is no evidence that Japanese fighters or bombers were involved and since so little damage was done it is virtually certain that the events of 'the Battle of Los Angeles' were not the result of enemy invasion.

WHAT REALLY HAPPENED?

The official explanation after the war was that meteorological balloons released over Los Angeles had been mistaken for enemy aircraft. It was certain that the targets at which the anti-aircraft units had fired were moving too slowly to have been Japanese planes. Once the firing had begun the smoke in the atmosphere made accurate identification more difficult and with the general air of panic it is not surprising that firing continued in spite of the lack of evidence of any actual enemy in the air.

The commander of the brigade in the area admitted that initially he thought he had seen 15 planes in the sky but soon realized that the smoke from the gunfire was misleading him. And some witnesses who saw the intensive gunfire said that they could never distinguish the shape of an aircraft. It is also curious that the 'planes' made no attempt to bomb the area, even though it contained valuable military installations. Stimson's suggestion that the aircraft were engaged in reconnaissance is plausible but is unsupported by any evidence. The failure of the majority of witnesses to observe any indisputable signs of planes makes that theory highly unlikely.

Another suggested explanation is that what the witnesses saw was a secret Japanese weapon called the Fu-Go Bombing Balloon. These devices certainly existed but were not launched against the

United States until 1944. According to Japanese records, design work on them did not even begin until late 1942, so they could not have been used in the 'attack' on Los Angeles.

The concept of balloons as long-range weapons is older than the Japanese weapons, with a British study into their effectiveness being commissioned as early as 1937. Operation Outward, as it was known, was approved in late 1941 and launched its first offensive balloons in March 1942, continuing until the D-Day landings and ending completely in September 1944. There is no evidence that the Japanese used balloons in war before the Fu-Go project in late 1942 but it is not impossible that they may have done so.

The idea that the situation resulted entirely from panic following the Ellwood raid is hard to reconcile with the fact that an object was detected by radar operators. It seemed to be coming from the Pacific and was moving slowly towards the land. This was soon followed by reports of Japanese planes being sighted over California. The artillery fire was a result of this state of panic as the US was unprepared for an enemy attack and the anti-aircraft units shot wildly at the presumed invaders without any success. There were 'reports' of Japanese planes having crashed as a result of this firing but subsequent investigation showed that they were mistaken.

It is difficult to imagine that even such a major misidentification could have led to anti-aircraft fire lasting for an hour and a half. War nerves and smoke from the anti-aircraft fire played a part in creating the event and the situation was not helped by contradictory stories from the military and the different theories put forward to explain it by government spokesmen. With such genuine confusion, possibly coupled with deliberate disinformation, it is hardly surprising that conspiracy theorists have become involved in the story.

POPULAR MYTHS

One of the most popular myths about the events of that day is that the craft seen in the sky resembled a giant butterfly. The original source for this story is claimed to have been an article in the *Reno Evening Gazette* of 26 February 1942 with the headline: 'Los Angeles Confused Over Air Raid Alarm'. A careful study of the news item shows that at no point was any mention made of a 'giant butterfly' being seen. This claim was not put forward until the 1960s, following the 'Mothman' UFO sightings (there were various reports of a man-sized flying creature in West Virginia at the time), with the events in 1942 being directly compared with the later ones. Since the *Reno Evening Gazette* makes no mention of any kind of giant butterfly, that theory can safely be ignored. Neither the media of the time nor eyewitnesses of the events described such a phenomenon.

Another myth about the 'battle' is that no attempt was made to scramble aircraft to investigate and take action against any enemy intruder. Nearly an hour passed between the initial air raid alert and the beginning of anti-aircraft fire. The planes, in fact, were on the runways and ready to go into action but there were not many fighter aircraft in the area and the decision was made to await developments before committing them to possible aerial combat.

EARLY US RADAR

Radar is another curious aspect of the events. Officially the US did not possess a radar system at the time of the raid but a government document dated 1983 claims that some form of radar was in existence as early as 1942. It was certainly not as advanced as later radar systems but it shows that many secret weapons were available to both sides during the war at a much earlier date than previously believed.

The radar system in use at the time was an SCR-268. This system allegedly had a range of only 22 miles (35 km) yet the mystery object was detected on radar at a distance of 120 miles (193 km) from Los Angeles.

The logical explanation for this discrepancy is that US radar was more sophisticated and powerful than the authorities were willing to admit to the public. If the range of SCR-268 really had been only 22 miles it would have been impossible for radar operators to have identified the object at a much greater distance than their acknowledged capability.

MOST LIKELY EXPLANATION

What are we to make of this strange affair? Clearly 'war nerves' and the Ellwood attack played a part. Even the armed forces appeared confused and gave contradictory accounts of the events of that day.

The most significant fact in all of the eyewitness stories is that the anti-aircraft battery that was closest to the phenomenon chose not to open fire. They clearly recognized that whatever they saw was not a hostile aircraft and so made no attempt to shoot it down. Other battalions with an inferior view of the 'craft' panicked and began firing. The presence of balloons in the area, together with a 'charged' atmosphere among the civilian population, is the most likely explanation for the strange events that have become known as 'the Battle of Los Angeles'.

CHAPTER TWO
THE BEER–CELLAR BOMBING

CHAPTER TWO

On 8 November 1939, Hitler missed death by minutes when a bomb exploded in the beer cellar in Munich where he had just finished speaking, killing eight people.

The events of that evening have been disputed ever since. There is no doubt that a live and primed time bomb was planted and set to explode while Hitler was speaking. What remains unclear, though, is who was behind the assassination attempt.

One of the most important dates in the Nazi calendar was 8 November. Every year Hitler came to Munich to address old party comrades who had been with him on that date in 1923. The meeting commemorated Hitler's unsuccessful attempt at a putsch – a violent takeover of the government – and those who died during its failure.

Thousands of people attended the annual ceremony and Hitler always addressed them for around an hour. It was one event he never missed and after his speech he was in the habit of talking over old times with former comrades for around half an hour before leaving.

Things went differently this year. September 1939 saw the beginning of World War II but the only fighting had been the brief war against Poland. Britain and France had not struck a blow in anger and the uneasy lull in hostilities led to this period becoming nicknamed the 'Phoney War'.

There was no prospect of imminent conflict. Germany was not being bombed by the RAF nor were its troops fighting the British and the French. So there were no pressing military reasons to prevent Hitler from continuing the habit of many years by reminiscing with old party comrades.

When Hitler had given his usual speech he left unexpectedly early. This meant that he was no longer present in the beer cellar when a large bomb exploded. Eight people were killed but Hitler was not one of them.

He would normally have flown back from the meeting to Berlin but that evening he took the train. His decision saved his life and ever since it has provoked a number of conspiracy theories about the events of that evening.

There are a number of indisputable facts about that night and perhaps that is the best place to begin. The bomb was planted in the beer cellar by a Communist artisan, Georg Elser. He had been a Marxist for many years and even when the Nazis came to power and the Communist Party was banned he continued to hold fast to his views. If anything, he became more convinced that the Nazis were treating the German workers unfairly.

No one denies that Elser built and planted the bomb. What has been disputed is whether he acted alone. If he had accomplices, who were they and what were their motives?

Throughout the 1920s and early 1930s political allegiances in Germany were volatile. Nazis and Communists in particular joined each other's movements and then switched sides, sometimes several times. Both parties drew most of their support from the working classes and the unemployed and even after Hitler came to power many Communists joined the Nazis. This was not simply out of a desire to 'infiltrate', although that played a part with some individuals. Mainly it arose from a genuine conviction that National Socialism, like Communism, represented a way out of poverty for the working classes. The membership of the SA was disproportionately made up of the unemployed and on becoming chancellor Hitler adopted a mixture of stick and carrot to hold on to power. As well as using the Gestapo and concentration camps to intimidate the working classes into obedience he knew that he needed to woo them into supporting or at least tolerating his rule.

He did this by devoting considerable money and resources to keeping German workers well fed, healthy and reasonably happy. On the whole the strategy worked, particularly before 1941. There were of course exceptions – Jews and Gypsies were singled out for persecution – but most people were left alone. Some Communist

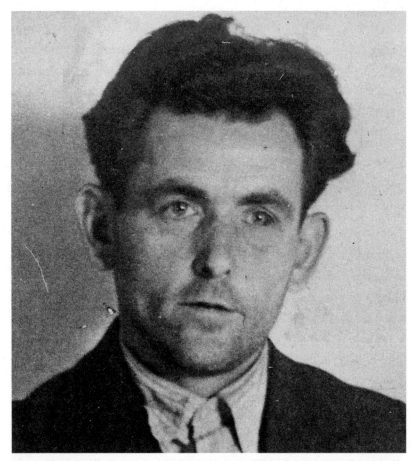

Georg Elser, the carpenter who tried to assassinate Hitler by planting a bomb in the Bürgerbraükeller, Munich in 1939 – he had always voted for the Communists.

leaders came to an accommodation with the regime and active resistance to the Nazis, even in the early years of power, was rare.

The Communist Party virtually disappeared as an organized body after 1933, although small cells remained. They were almost completely ineffective until the last year of the war and confined their activities principally to talking.

PLANTING THE BOMB

One former Communist who felt differently was the carpenter Georg Elser. He was not a particularly active party member before 1933, but he had always voted for the Communists and seems to have kept in touch with a few like-minded individuals even after the Nazis came to power.

In 1938 Elser decided that only an act of terrorism could bring about change. He made up his mind that Hitler had to be assassinated and that he was the man to carry out the plan.

Elser began his preparations by stealing explosives from the arms factory where he worked. He acquired 250 packets of gunpowder through this process. At that time he was not certain how he would carry out his plan to assassinate Hitler but on reading a newspaper announcement about the forthcoming commemoration of Hitler's failed putsch on 8 and 9 November he saw an opportunity.

Knowing that Hitler never missed the event, Elser travelled to Munich. He inspected the beer hall and made a careful note of any possible methods of planting a bomb. Elser decided that the ideal place to conceal his explosives was in a pillar immediately behind the rostrum where Hitler spoke. He knew that the bomb would have to be detonated by a clockwork timer rather than a fuse.

In April 1939 Elser returned to the beer cellar and made detailed measurements. From August onwards he laboured night after night on the pillar, removing a 2.62-foot square section of the wooden panelling. He worked on his hands and knees to hollow it out and disposed of the rubble after each session. Each night he hid in the beer cellar until it was locked up for the night and then began his long and laborious task.

By early morning on 6 November 1939 he had completed his preparations. The bomb was ready and Elser set the timer for 9.20 p.m. on 8 November. He made a final inspection on the night of 7 November before taking a train to Constance in Switzerland.

Events then began to conspire against him. Half an hour before the explosion took place he was stopped by two customs officials. His border crossing pass was out of date so the guards conducted a search. They found in his pockets a postcard of the beer cellar, addresses of ammunition factories, some bolts, screws and springs and his Communist Party badge. They still had no idea who he was or what he had done, but he was taken to the police station for further interrogation. It was there, at midnight, when the radio announced the news of the assassination attempt and ordered frontier guards to be on full alert, that it finally dawned on them that Elser might be a suspicious character. Even then they assumed he was either a deserter or a spy.

Hitler began his address at 8.10 p.m. and spoke for almost an hour, concluding his speech at 9.07 p.m. His normal practice was to remain behind and talk over old times with party veterans but tonight he left immediately after finishing his speech. At 9.20 p.m. the bomb exploded, killing eight people and injuring over 60.

WERE THE BRITISH INVOLVED?

The events of that night have launched a number of conspiracy theories of varying degrees of plausibility. Nazi Germany's leaders were paranoid throughout their rule, but the explosion in the beer cellar led them to formulate the earliest – and most generally dismissed – conspiratorial view of Elser's bomb plot.

Hitler and Himmler refused to believe that a lone bomber was responsible. They were convinced that there must have been a wider conspiracy involving the British Secret Service and the dissident Nazi Otto Strasser, safely in exile but still a bitter enemy.

The consensus among historians is that this notion was at best a paranoid fantasy or, perhaps more probably, deliberate propaganda. An examination of the 'Venlo Incident' and particularly its aftermath indicates that perhaps there was an element of truth in these Nazi claims.

For some months two British agents, Major Richard Stevens and Captain Sigismund Payne Best, had been based in Holland. They were negotiating with Franz Fischer, a Nazi spy who pretended to be a political refugee. Fischer claimed to be in touch with anti-Nazi officers in the German Army who were planning a coup against Hitler. This was a deliberate deception on his part because he was working for the SS.

Walter Schellenberg, one of Himmler's most trusted aides, crossed into Holland and met with Best and Stevens. He pretended to be Captain Schaemmel and to be acting on behalf of a dissident German general.

At this stage Nazi intelligence was still playing 'the long game' and Schellenberg was on the verge of meeting the two agents again and introducing them to a fictitious general. However, Elser's bomb plot dramatically altered the SS plans.

Himmler immediately rang Schellenberg and ordered him to meet Best and Stevens the next day. They were to be arrested and brought back to Germany. Armed SS men would assist in the operation and the violation of the Dutch border was 'of no consequence', in Himmler's words. Schellenberg was unhappy and protested against the order, but when Himmler repeated his command he did not dare disobey. The British agents were captured in a lightning raid and imprisoned in a concentration camp.

The capture of Best and Stevens was a disaster for British intelligence. Networks that had been painstakingly built up were smashed and agents were arrested or forced into hiding. In spite of the self-serving and self-justificatory tone of Best's account of the incident in his 1949 book, his actions come across as naïve, amateurish and incompetent.

DID STRASSER MASTERMIND THE PLOT?

Perhaps a sense of his failure led Best to formulate a conspiracy theory that, even though it was exploded as early as 1969, is still believed by many. Best claimed that while they were both prisoners in Sachsenhausen concentration camp the conveniently dead Elser had told him that he had been hired to kill dissident Nazis in return for 40,000 Swiss francs. This claim is a complete fabrication.

It is understandable that when Best published his book almost anything conspiratorial regarding the Nazis was believed. Alan Bullock's classic biography of Hitler came out in 1952 and with no alternative sources available to him he simply repeated Best's story. Later historians have no such excuse. Primary sources have been widely available since the early 1970s and show clearly that whether or not Elser acted alone – a question that will be examined in its turn – he certainly did *not* have Nazi accomplices and was *not* in the pay of the Nazis.

To add to the confusion Best also kept an unpublished diary, which gives strikingly different accounts of his movements and other aspects of the time. His wife's own diary also contradicts statements made in her husband's unpublished journal. For example, he claims that Elser was a member of Strasser's Black

Front (a dissident political group), which has been shown repeatedly to be false. He also maintains that Elser met Strasser in Switzerland, when in fact the movements of both men have been traced in detail, proving that at no time did they meet, in Switzerland or elsewhere. Best claims that Strasser was the mastermind of the plot and that he and Elser liaised to make it possible. None of this tissue of fantasy appeared in Best's book, *The Venlo Incident*, probably because Strasser was still alive and could have disproved the claims.

The idea that Best is any kind of trustworthy 'source' of information about Elser is simply impossible to sustain. He is caught out in contradictions and lies on numerous occasions and everything he wrote is essentially pure fiction and is not to be taken seriously.

The question remains – why did Best lie about Elser? Only two reasons suggest themselves. One is that the British agent was trying to cover up his incompetence and the other is that he was trying to cover up British involvement in the bomb plot. There is little direct evidence for British involvement, but it is more plausible than is generally believed. The probability is that Elser's plot was not the result of Secret Service involvement but the possibility has been dismissed far too easily.

The notion that Elser's bomb plot was 'staged' by the Nazis is contradicted by all the documentary evidence. It rests on a combination of statements that are factually false and others that are based on incorrect assumptions.

One of the most common 'false facts' about the evening of 8 November 1939 is the frequently repeated statement that Hitler's speech was shorter than usual and that he spoke more rapidly than normal. That is simply false, as eyewitnesses testified. And the fact that Hitler left immediately after speaking rather than remaining to talk to old comrades is claimed to show prior knowledge of the explosion.

In reality there are two perfectly rational explanations for his early departure. One is that the war, though still largely in the 'phoney' stage, needed attention and Hitler was contemplating an imminent invasion of France. The other is the weather. It was Hitler's practice to fly back to Berlin from Munich but the thick fog made flying impossible. He did not stay behind because a train from Munich to Berlin was due to leave shortly and he wanted to return that night and resume planning the invasion.

Another aspect of Elser's bombing which conspiracy theorists seize on as evidence of the plot being a Nazi 'false flag' is the appalling lack of security at the beer cellar, even on the night of Hitler's speech. The explanation for that is not any kind of Nazi conspiracy but the fact that security for this particular event was always left in the hands of the 'Old Fighters'. The chief of security was Christian Weber, a brutal thug who had been given the task of supervising security at the beer cellar by Hitler. But by 1939, six years of living high on the hog had turned Weber into a lazy and pleasure-loving clown who simply could not be bothered to carry out his duties properly. This indifference allowed Elser to spend 35 nights working on the bomb in the beer cellar without ever being disturbed or challenged by police, security guards or the SS. Not a single security check had been carried out by Weber and his laxity nearly led to Hitler's death. It must never be forgotten that he escaped being killed by less than 15 minutes. No Nazi plot would have risked so fine a margin of error.

The idea that Otto Strasser was behind the plot has been put forward by several people and it was certainly proclaimed at the time by Nazi propagandists. There is no doubt that Strasser would have been delighted to see Hitler dead, but he was an impotent figure who was exiled and in fear of his life and with almost no support within Germany. He might well have wanted to see Elser's plot succeed but there is not the slightest evidence that he was involved in it at any stage – planning or execution. That particular idea was simply Nazi paranoia fixing on an obvious suspect but with no basis in fact. Strasser himself denied any involvement in Elser's bombing.

DID ELSER ACT ALONE?

Another theory is that Elser was part of a three-man Communist Party cell. There is no doubt that Elser was a party member and had always voted Communist. On the other hand he had a reputation as a 'loner' and for the type of task he was planning it would be extremely dangerous to recruit allies. Nor, given his skills as a carpenter and clockmaker, did he need any accomplices.

Two names are mentioned as being Elser's co-conspirators – Karl Kuch and a waiter known simply as Ketterer. There is no doubt that Kuch existed and was a Communist but beyond that there is little evidence for his involvement in any kind of bomb plot. Various figures claim that Kuch and Elser knew each other and met frequently; others deny that they ever met. The evidence from public records is conclusive; Kuch and Elser never met and were *not* involved in any joint conspiracy to assassinate Hitler. Ketterer the waiter is equally elusive and Kuch's death in a car crash while trying to flee to Switzerland was not because of the bomb plot – which was still months down the line – but because his Communist sympathies had been discovered by the Gestapo. Yet another conspiracy theory has been woven out of whole cloth.

The Gestapo were both ruthless and thorough in their attempts to persuade Elser to talk about his 'accomplices' but under torture he persisted in claiming that he had worked alone. Hypnosis also produced the same answer and even doses of the 'truth drug' still led to his stubborn insistence that he had acted alone.

Elser admitted that he had 'talked' with various people whom he claimed he did not know and had expressed his dissatisfaction with National Socialism. However, he had never broached the subject of the assassination of Hitler with anyone and had acted entirely without accomplices.

Himmler personally interrogated Elser and tried to force him to name names but even he eventually had to accept that the German carpenter was telling the truth. For propaganda purposes, the media were told that Britain and Otto Strasser had masterminded the plot, but Himmler, like every senior Nazi, knew the reality. One brave man had stood alone against the Nazi tyranny and had decided – knowing that it would probably cost him his life – that there was no alternative but to plant his bomb at the November commemoration ceremony in Munich.

It is possible that Elser may have been trying to protect people he knew but the fact that even the administration of drugs failed to elicit a different story from him is testimony to the truth of what he had been saying. This simple working man was a true hero of the German Resistance and his failed attempt could have saved the lives of millions who died needlessly. Many years after his death he was eventually honoured by Germany for his deeds.

CHAPTER THREE
MYSTERIOUS DEATHS

GLENN MILLER: A MUSICIAN'S DISAPPEARANCE

Glenn Miller was the most successful band leader of his era. Dubbed 'the King of Swing', he was at the height of his fame when in 1942 he disbanded his orchestra and joined the Army Specialist Corps. Later that year Miller was transferred to the Army Air Force. He proceeded to introduce swing music into military marches.

Miller created a new orchestra and began giving concerts to troops. On 20 March 1943, the 418th Army Air Force band gave its first performance. He was desperate to play to American service personnel overseas and eventually received permission. His now British-based band was enthusiastically welcomed by the troops. Lieutenant General James Doolittle told him: 'Next to a letter from home your orchestra is the greatest morale-booster in the European theater of operations.'

In 1942, band leader Glenn Miller, 'King of Swing', joined the Army Specialist Corps and started playing for the troops. But one day, his plane, which was bound for France, just disappeared...

Miller and his band played concerts in airfields and aircraft hangars and performed on the American Forces Network. They even appeared on a show called *The Wehrmacht Hour*, which mixed swing music with propaganda. Apparently, Miller struggled to speak German for the programme.

Miller's first address in London was 25 Sloane Court, but this area was a favourite target of the V-1 doodlebugs, so he decided to relocate the orchestra to Bedford, north of London. Next day, a V-1 crashed in front of their former lodgings, destroying the building and killing over a hundred people. Miller's response was: 'As long as the Miller luck stays with us, we have nothing to worry about.'

When Miller and his band were playing at an open-air performance in Kent, the sound of V-1s was heard overhead. The audience dived for cover, but Miller and his orchestra continued playing. After the explosion, the audience returned and gave them a standing ovation.

Miller's workload was intense and demanding. In one month he played 35 live concerts and made 46 broadcasts.

Weary though he was, Miller wanted to perform for the troops in France. In late 1944, it was agreed that he and his band could move to Paris and play a concert on Christmas Day.

On 15 November, the band's manager was given permission to fly to Paris and make the arrangements. Then Miller announced that he wanted to go. The weather was extremely poor, with thick fog making flying difficult. This unfavourable weather grounded the Supreme Headquarters Allied Expeditionary Forces (SHAEF) shuttle on which he had planned to travel.

Then on 14 December, Miller met Lieutenant Colonel Norman Baessell, who was flying to Paris the following day in a UC-64A Norseman light aircraft. Baessell invited Miller to fly to France with him. It was raining heavily and visibility was poor, but the plane still took off. It was never seen again. Miller, Baessell and the pilot all vanished without a trace.

No one knew Miller was missing until 18 December because he had boarded the Norseman without permission or the knowledge of senior officers. A board of inquiry was set up by the 8th Air Force which concluded that the Norseman had been lost in the English Channel. Bad weather, pilot error and possible engine failure were the probable causes.

Conspiracy theories

That was the official verdict but later on conspiracy theories were put forward. The German journalist Udo Ulfkotte told *Bild* newspaper in 1997 that he had 'secret evidence' that Miller had never boarded the Norseman at all. Instead, he had flown to Paris the previous day and had died of a heart attack in a Paris brothel. The official version of his death was a cover-up to protect Miller's reputation. Later Ulfkotte admitted that he had no 'evidence' for his claims, which were based on information received from German intelligence sources.

Retired US colonel Hunton Downs came up with another conspiracy theory. He claimed that Miller was a 'superspy' for the OSS – forerunner of the CIA – and that he had died on an undercover mission. Downs claimed that Miller's mission was to contact German generals and persuade them to overthrow Hitler. However, the plan had failed and Miller was captured. After being tortured, he was killed by the Nazis and his corpse was dumped on the doorstep of a Paris brothel. The story of the Norseman's crash was invented to protect his reputation.

Miller's younger brother Herb said in 1983 that: 'Glenn Miller did not die in a plane crash over the Channel, but from lung cancer in a hospital.' According to him, Miller became so ill on the

Norseman that the pilot had to make an emergency landing. Miller was taken to a military hospital but died the next day. Herb Miller said that he dreamed up the story of a crash in the Channel to let his brother be remembered as a hero.

Miller was certainly a heavy smoker and admitted that: 'I am totally emaciated, although I am eating enough.' Others remarked on how thin and ill he looked. Certainly, the idea that he might have died of lung cancer is plausible.

There are, however, several objections to this theory. The first is the question of time. Why did Herb Miller wait until 1983 before making his claim? Why is his version of Miller's death not confirmed by military records – US or British? And what would be the purpose of keeping his death in hospital a secret for so long?

Perhaps the most plausible of all the conspiracy theories surrounding Miller's death was put forward by Fred Shaw. Shaw was a former navigator in RAF Bomber Command who had served on an Avro Lancaster bomber which was returning from a failed raid on German railway yards. When the Lancaster approached the south coast of Britain, it was dropping its bombs over the official 'south jettison zone' when Shaw looked out and saw a Norseman flying beneath the plane. The rear gunner of the aircraft cried out: 'Did you see that kite [aircraft] go in?' In Shaw's opinion, it was the shock waves created by the explosion that downed the Norseman.

The Air Historical Branch of the Ministry of Defence neither confirmed nor denied Shaw's claims. Their response was to say that it was possible that the Norseman and the bomber could have crossed in flight.

The pilot of the Lancaster, Victor Gregory, partially confirmed Shaw's story. He admitted that he saw nothing but recalled both Shaw and the rear gunner saying that they had seen the Norseman.

Perhaps that is the true explanation of Glenn Miller's death – a tragic case of friendly fire. That would at least provide a motive for any cover-up. Whatever the truth about his fate, Miller's music lived on long after his death.

LESLIE HOWARD: DEATH OF AN ACTOR

The actor Leslie Howard was among the passengers on a civil aircraft flying from Lisbon to London on 1 June 1943. Howard had found fame and fortune in Hollywood playing Ashley Wilkes in *Gone with the Wind,* but he returned to Britain to serve his country. It was not in a military capacity but as a propagandist that he supported Britain's war effort. He starred in a number of morale-boosting films, most notably *First of the Few,* in which he played R. J. Mitchell, designer of the Spitfire.

Howard was not originally a passenger on the DC-3 from Portela (the airport for Lisbon). He and his business manager, Alfred Chenhalls, had replaced three other passengers who were taken off the plane. The take-off passed without incident and the civilian airliner continued its journey unmolested for the next two hours. However, there was a burst of Luftwaffe activity only a few minutes after the plane's departure from Portela, when eight Junkers Ju 88 C-6 fighters left their base at Bordeaux and flew westwards.

At 12.45 p.m. they saw the DC-3. There was bright sunshine and excellent visibility and the aircraft in their sights bore unmistakably civilian markings. It is therefore impossible for the German pilots to have imagined it to be a military plane.

In spite of the fact that they were clearly facing an unarmed passenger aircraft the Junkers attacked the plane. Its wireless operator sent a frantic message in Morse code to the RAF Signals Station at Whitchurch in Somerset. This message, sent at 12.54

p.m., was chilling. 'From G-AGBB [the aircraft's number] to GKH. Am being attacked by enemy aircraft.'

Then the transmission fell silent. The Ju fighters' attack had caused the fuel tanks to catch fire and the plane exploded. There were no survivors.

Given the impossibility of the Germans mistaking the airliner for a military plane, why did they shoot down the aircraft? It must have been premeditated as the Junkers squadron left Bordeaux only minutes after the DC-3 had taken off from Portugal.

Was Churchill the target?

What led the Luftwaffe to target this particular aircraft? There are several theories, all but one involving the passengers on board. Perhaps the most obvious is the one Churchill subscribed to, that the Germans believed he was travelling the plane.

Churchill had been visiting North Africa and the Germans were well aware of his presence there. As he put it in his *History of the Second World War*:

> This [his presence in North Africa] led to a tragedy which much distressed me. A thickset man smoking a cigar walked up and was thought to be a passenger upon it. The German Agency therefore signalled that I was on board.

In other words, the Germans shot down the aircraft because they believed that Churchill was a passenger. The man referred to by Churchill was Leslie Howard's business manager, Alfred Chenhalls, who bore a striking resemblance to him. If the Germans really believed that the prime minister was on the plane, they might have risked the odium of shooting down a civilian airliner in order to remove him from the scene.

Churchill certainly regarded this as the most likely explanation. He remarked contemptuously:

> *The brutality of the Germans was only matched by the stupidity of their agents. It is difficult to understand how anyone could imagine that, with all the resources of Great Britain at my disposal, I should have booked a passage in an unarmed and unescorted plane from Lisbon and flown home in broad daylight.*

Two German agents certainly looked at the passenger list of the fatal flight. They may well have imagined that 'Chenhalls' was a pseudonym for Churchill. When they physically observed a man who resembled him boarding the plane, they could have alerted the German High Command to the possibility that Churchill might be among the passengers.

Another possibility is that Howard was the intended target. His propaganda film *Pimpernel Smith* had infuriated Goebbels. He was certainly on the Nazi 'hit list' and his Jewish ancestry would have given them an additional motive to seek his death.

Two other passengers would also have been Nazi targets. One was Wilfrid Israel, an exiled German Jew. Israel helped smuggle thousands of Jews to safety and had flown to Portugal to help Jewish refugees there and in Spain find sanctuary in Palestine. Israel also recruited many German Jewish scientists to work on the Manhattan Project, the American atomic bomb programme.

Ivan Sharp was another possible Nazi target. He was an industrialist charged by the British government with buying up tungsten at inflated prices to prevent the Germans from obtaining it. The Nazis would have wished to eliminate him as he was a thorn in their side.

The final possibility is that the plane was shot down as the result of a tragic accident. There is no doubt that Ju 88s patrolled the Bay of Biscay area to provide air cover for U-boats. On the fateful afternoon, the Junkers squadron were out on patrol looking for two submarines which they planned to escort to safety. The weather was poor, so they called off the search and instead patrolled the area around them.

Then at 12.45 p.m., they spotted the DC-3. Five minutes later they prepared to attack it. They could not distinguish any markings but could tell by the shape and construction of the aircraft that it was not German, so they fired on the plane from above and below which set the port engine and wing on fire.

At that point the squadron leader realized it was a civilian aircraft and called off the attack, but it was too late. The aircraft crashed into the sea and sank.

This is the version of events given by three surviving pilots who had been involved in the shooting. It is quite possible that they panicked and fired out of fear. Ju 88s were notoriously slow and they might have shot first and regretted their actions later.

There are, however, problems with that explanation. For months civilian airliners had been leaving Portugal and flying to Britain over the same route without any attempt being made to attack them. The DC-3's civilian status was clearly evidenced by its markings and the weather was not poor but sunny. Also, agents in Portugal had certainly told the Abwehr [German military intelligence] that they thought Churchill might be on the plane and the Junkers squadron was scrambled only minutes after the DC-3 took off.

The truth will never be known but the strong probability is that the airliner was deliberately shot down because the Germans believed that Churchill was on board. Leslie Howard and the other passengers almost certainly died as the result of a case of mistaken identity.

THE MYSTERY OF THE MURDERED REDHEAD

During World War II, most of Europe was occupied by the Germans. The neutral countries – Spain, Portugal, Switzerland and Sweden – became hotbeds of intrigue and espionage. Sweden was particularly important because its geographical position meant that German, Soviet and British agents could operate there relatively freely.

In this atmosphere the glamorous socialite Jane Horney – born Ebba Charlotta Horney – became a key player. Even her origins are in dispute. One version claims that she was born in Stockholm, while another story makes her an illegitimate child born in Scotland and adopted by her Swedish father and Danish mother.

A tall and striking redhead and considered a beauty by men, Jane Horney had a husband and numerous lovers. Her husband was a journalist for the pro-Nazi paper *Aftonbladet*, but they divorced after two years of marriage.

After her divorce she became part of the Swedish social scene and embarked on a series of affairs, the majority of them with diplomats or servicemen. Many of them were spies.

Jane Horney had no inhibitions about trading sex for secrets. She had affairs with British, German and Russian diplomats and military staff as well as members of the Danish Resistance. Each group she came into contact with suspected her of working for one of the others.

Among her lovers were Ronald Turnbull, a Special Operations Executive (SOE); Otto Danielsson and Martin Lundqvist of Swedish military intelligence; the Russian agent Alexander Pavlov; Jørgen Winkel, a member of the Danish Resistance; Karl-Heinz Hoffmann, head of the Gestapo in Denmark; and Hermann Seibold, who ran German counter-intelligence operations in Scandinavia.

Even more intriguing among the list of Horney's many lovers is Horst Gilbert. He worked for the Abwehr in Denmark and reported to Admiral Canaris. Both men were secret anti-Nazis and either or both may have been playing a double game. Gilbert was friendly with Alexandra Kollontai, the Soviet ambassador to Sweden. He contacted her and asked if it would be possible to conclude a separate peace with the Soviet Union.

Horney travelled through an underground Danish Resistance 'shuttle' to meet Gilbert in Copenhagen. She did this on numerous occasions. Somehow she obtained a pass allowing her to travel freely within the occupied countries and visited Germany several times. On her return to Sweden she passed on any information she had acquired to Swedish intelligence.

In March 1944 she began a liaison with a British agent whose identity remains unknown. For several months they conducted an affair which, on her side at least, was passionate. She declared that she was in love with him and when he broke off their relationship she was heartbroken.

For some weeks she hid herself away before re-emerging and beginning an affair with a German agent. The Danish Resistance were becoming increasingly suspicious of her and she was shadowed, photographed and eventually reported by them to the Swedish authorities as a possible Nazi agent. The Secret Service in Sweden then arrested her and she was interrogated by them for three weeks.

The Swedish authorities finally cleared her of any wrongdoing and told the Danish Resistance members that she was not a traitor. Outwardly they accepted that verdict but privately refused to believe that Horney was not a German spy so they decided to murder her.

Was she murdered?

What happened next has never been fully established. Clearly, Horney knew secrets that more than one intelligence agency did not wish to be revealed.

All that is known for certain about her next move is that two members of the Danish Resistance approached her and persuaded her to go to Copenhagen to clear herself of the suspicions against her. She agreed and on 16 February 1945 she and her female friend Bodil Frederiksen accompanied the two men to Malmö. They checked into the Grand Hotel, the two women staying in adjacent rooms. They were joined there by another member of the Danish Resistance, a student called Hjalmar Ravnbo.

The following night she left the hotel at 10 p.m. with Frederiksen and Ravnbo. From that point onwards her fate is conjectural. The probability is that the Danish Resistance shot her dead and wrapped her body in iron chains before throwing her into the sea to sink.

After the war was over her father demanded an investigation into her disappearance but the Swedish police enquiries met with total silence. The Danish and Swedish secret services closed their files on her and British intelligence claimed never to have heard of her. Even former German operatives who had been her lovers refused to speak about her. The Swedish police, possibly to their relief, were then forced to abandon their enquiries.

It is difficult to explain the lack of rigour in prosecuting the case or the wall of silence and outright denials which the police encountered, except on the basis of a cover-up. There might be several motives for such behaviour – the fear of exposing agents or anxiety that information which was still secret might be revealed during the investigation. Another explanation could be that Horney had discovered a traitor within the Danish Resistance who murdered her to protect his or her identity.

Frederiksen is an enigma. She was active in the Danish Resistance and accompanied Horney at least as far as Malmö. Both women were red-haired and there was a striking physical resemblance between them which sometimes led to them being confused with one another.

Did she switch identities?

The fact that Frederiksen and Horney looked extremely similar has led to a conspiracy theory alleging that the two women changed clothes and switched identities. If that had indeed been the case, Horney could have been the woman seen boarding the train from Malmö to Stockholm while Frederiksen was the woman murdered in the fishing boat.

Is it possible that Horney feared the Danish Resistance and persuaded Frederiksen to assume her identity? If she did so, was she knowingly sending the other woman to her death? Is it possible that it was Frederiksen rather than Horney who was the traitor?

Another theory also assumes a switch of clothes and a transfer of identities but this time without any fatal consequences. It suggests that Horney was smuggled out of Sweden while Frederiksen pretended to be her, managing to make her way safely to Denmark before returning home under her true identity.

There is also a conspiracy theory which maintains that Horney was never murdered at all but that her death was faked to throw other intelligence agencies off the scent. She was then smuggled into Britain where she began spying against the Russians on behalf of MI6.

In 1947 one of the two Danish Resistance fighters who had persuaded Horney to go back to Denmark spoke up. Asbjørn Lyhne confessed to Swedish police that he had been involved in her murder. There was no supporting evidence and as he soon withdrew his confession the police released him.

No one knows the truth about Jane Horney. Was she murdered or did she switch identities with Bodil Frederiksen? If she was murdered, why? Did she escape to safety? Did she turn her wartime espionage talents to the Cold War and serve MI6?

Whatever the answer may be, her disappearance and probable murder remains a fascinating mystery that remains unsolved and probably always will.

THE VELSER AFFAIR: TREASON OR MISADVENTURE?

In the dying stages of the war in Europe, several members of the Dutch Communist Resistance were killed by the Nazis. The charismatic Resistance fighter Hannie Schaft was shot dead in the dunes of Bloemendaal only three weeks before Holland was liberated.

There were rumours at the time that have never been proved or disproved, involving a deliberate conspiracy by elements in the Dutch police to hand over various people, mainly members of the Communist Resistance, to the Nazis. The intention was to prevent them from forming the nucleus of a possible Communist takeover in the Netherlands.

Two inquiries into the case were reluctantly undertaken before being abandoned as 'not in the national interest'. Then in 1951 Commissioner W. J. Gorten led a new inquiry but an unknown assailant fired shots at him.

Conny Braam, who grew up in Velsen – the scene of the alleged betrayals – described the atmosphere in the town following these events. She wrote:

> *People were afraid. One police officer who attempted to investigate the affair was removed from the case in the 1950s*

and another one got a bullet fired through his window. In Velsen they always say, if you want to live a long time, keep your mouth shut about the affair.

Holland, like every occupied country in Europe, produced some people who actively resisted the Nazis and others who collaborated with them. Once the Netherlands was liberated, a wave of reprisals against collaborators took place. Some were vigilante punishments, but the Dutch authorities also arrested many people.

Police collaboration

One of the accusations made in the 'Velser Affair' is that some of the police officers in charge of punishing collaborators had themselves been guilty of collaboration. Many had joined the Resistance and become leaders within it and the claim is that some of them used their positions in the Resistance to betray Jews, Communists and left-wingers to the Nazis.

Between December 1945 and January 1946, an investigation was launched into the conduct of Dutch police officers and some members of the Resistance. Some of the people undertaking the inquiry were themselves accused of having been part of the 'Velser Affair'. Leo Rodrigues Lopes, the editor-in-chief of *De Ochtendpost* (Morning Post), submitted a document to the authorities in Amsterdam and requested the minister of justice to set up an independent inquiry rather than leaving it in the hands of the 'Special Appeal'.

In his article in *De Ochtendpost* Lopes accused Chief Inspector J. P. Engels and Commissioner J. P. Weyburg of handing over RAF personnel to the Germans. He also alleged that Velsen police officers had arrested Jews and handed them over to the Nazis, often stealing their assets. They also arrested Communists and illegal workers and sometimes even gave orders for people to be murdered. Some of those involved were also part of the team investigating crimes after the liberation of Holland and used their positions to cover up their wartime activities. In July 1946, Lopes was warned by one of his junior editors that a phone call had threatened him with 'a shot in the neck' if he did not stop publishing articles on the subject.

Two separate investigations were carried out at the same time. One was headed by Nico Sikkel, deputy prosecutor at the Amsterdam Court of Appeal and the other was conducted by Prosecutor General van Thiel, also of the Amsterdam Court of Appeal. Neither shared information or co-operated in any way. However, the enquiries they made were soon shelved and transferred to other people.

Sikkel has been particularly accused of corruption. His brother-in-law was the prime minister of the Netherlands and it has been alleged that he charged Sikkel with the task of ridding Holland of communism. Sikkel is also accused of making secret deals to betray Communist fighters in the Resistance to the Germans during the last stages of the war.

There is no doubt that negotiations took place between the Bureau of Intelligence and Nazi officers concerning German dossiers on Dutch Communists. The most recent author on the subject, Bas von Benda-Beckmann, wrote in his book *De Velser Affaire*: 'At the end of the war there was a panic feeling. Communist members of the Resistance would withhold arms for Communist Resistance with the aim of a putsch, a takeover of power.'

Of all the writers on the Velser Affair, Benda-Beckmann is one of the few who does not view it as a conspiracy. He wrote: 'There was a tense atmosphere, but this was not reflected in a concentrated campaign to eliminate as many Communist resistors as possible.' Benda-Beckmann believes the increasing Nazi desperation, recklessness on the part of some members of the Resistance and perhaps a greater willingness to protect non-Communist resistors were the main reasons why a small number of Communist partisans were killed by the Nazis.

Schaft meets her death

There is no doubt that some police officers were in contact with Resistance groups. Two important Resistance centres were the Westerveld Cemetery and the Velsen Crematorium. The dunes around the town were also favourite hiding places of Resistance fighters and it was there that the charismatic Hannie Schaft met her death.

Schaft was one of the most attractive characters in the Dutch Resistance. She began her work by stealing identity cards for Jewish residents of Holland and joined the Raad van Verzet (Council of Resistance) group. This was closely tied to the Dutch Communist Party, though its members were not exclusively Communists.

Before long Schaft wanted to become actively involved. She was a crack shot and carried out a number of acts of sabotage and assassination. Her victims were Germans and collaborators and as she spoke fluent German she was able to fraternize with the enemy soldiers.

She had her own moral code, which led her to refuse some assignments. When she was asked to kidnap the children of a Nazi officer she flatly refused on the grounds that she was not willing to risk the lives of children. She became known to the Nazis as 'the girl with the red hair' and she was soon on the 'most wanted' list posted by the Nazis.

Aware of her new notoriety, she dyed her hair black and once more began her campaign of sabotage and assassination. She also transported weapons and distributed illegal newspapers.

Her career came to an end on 21 March 1945 when she was arrested at a military checkpoint in Haarlem. She was distributing the Communist newspaper *De Waarheid* (The Truth). After being tortured, she was eventually identified by the red roots of her hair and on 17 April 1945 she was murdered.

Murdered by Dutch collaborators

It was not the German occupying forces but Dutch Nazi collaborators who killed her. An agreement had been made between the German occupiers and the Binnelandse Strijdkrachten to stop any further executions, but in spite of that she was taken to the dunes of Bloemendaal by two collaborators. The first man shot her at close range but only wounded her, prompting the scornful riposte: 'I shoot better than you.' The second man then delivered the fatal shot.

The murder of Schaft was perhaps the single most bitterly condemned action of the last stages of the war in Holland. Almost immediately the police were accused of complicity in her death.

It's possible that there was some degree of 'leaking' information to the Germans and maybe the Nazis were increasingly aware of the Resistance locations. A mixture of both might have played a part in the various events that have become known as the 'Velser Affair'.

Benda-Beckmann and retired police officer Guus Hartendorf have written the two most meticulously researched books on the case. Hartendorf sees evidence of at least partial truth in the accusations while Benda-Beckmann believes that there was no conspiracy.

Even so, Benda-Beckmann concludes by saying: 'I do not dare to say whether the discussion is over.'

MASS GRAVES AT MALBORK

Malbork in Poland was known for centuries as Marienburg. It was a wholly German city and had been part of Prussia for hundreds of years. During the Soviet advance in 1945, most of the civilian population fled, but 4,000 either decided to remain or could not escape to safety. The city saw fierce fighting between German and Soviet soldiers and on 9 March 1945 it was captured by Russian troops. Following its occupation by the Red Army, its civilian population vanished and 1,840 people remain unaccounted for.

In June 1945 Marienburg was handed over to Polish Communists. They promptly renamed it Malbork and expelled the tiny number of Germans who had not already died in the fighting or fled.

That was the end of the story until 1996. In that year, 178 bodies were discovered in a mass grave and in 2005 a further 123 were found. In October 2008, a huge burial site was found that contained the bodies of 2,116 people, nearly all of them female. Each one of them was identified as a German resident of the city.

A Polish investigation quickly decided that they may have died either of disease or during the fighting and that their bodies were buried to prevent the spread of typhus. On 14 August 2009, the bodies were buried in a German military cemetery to the west of the town.

This cosy explanation by the Polish investigators is not shared by everyone. In particular, government officials in Malbork stated that they believed they had been the victims of a massacre. Piotr Szwedowski, a city official, said that one in ten of the corpses had been shot in the head. He added that they had been buried naked, 'without shoes, without clothes, without personal items. The metal detectors used during the excavations found no metal, not even a false tooth.' Szwedowski did, however, believe that some had died of natural causes such as extreme cold or the artillery bombardment of the town.

One of the workmen excavating the site expressed his distress at finding so many bodies of dead children. 'At first we were constantly finding children's skeletons,' he said, 'and that was really hard for me. I have a young son myself.'

Neither Polish nor German documents make any mention of the grave. The conclusion of the Polish authorities is that it must have been dug during the period between March and May 1945, when the city was occupied by Soviet troops. Maciej Schulz of the Institute of National Remembrance states that it was standard practice for Red Army soldiers to strip bodies and bury them in bomb craters.

How did they die?

How these people met their deaths remains controversial. Cold and disease and the ravages of the fierce fighting certainly must have played a part. But Bodo Rückert, the head of an association of Germans expelled from Malbork, whose own family left the town during the final stages of the war, believes they may have been murdered by Poles as an act of revenge against the German occupiers. Perhaps more obvious suspects are the Red Army, who were in control of the town for three months and who were certainly not shy about exacting revenge on Germans when they captured territory from them. Polish officials have been searching their own archives and have also asked Russian archivists to search their records, but the Russians have failed to respond to the Polish request.

There was fierce fighting between German and Russian troops and cold and disease would certainly have led to illness and death. On the other hand, when the German Army left the town, there were still a few thousand civilians left alive. Only around a thousand were deported when the Poles took over in May.

The bodies discovered were all naked and mainly female, but only 10 per cent of them showed signs of bullet wounds. A Pole who entered the city as a child after the Russian conquest described seeing: 'German prisoners in torn uniforms, guarded by Russian soldiers, driving around the city in an old truck and collecting the decaying bodies from the streets'. He added that he had only seen around 300 dead bodies, which were all those of soldiers – German and Russian – and that they had been 'dumped at the foot of the castle hill'.

It is highly probable that Russian soldiers stripped the bodies and burned their clothes and also looted any possessions. To what extent the more than 2,000 corpses can be accounted for on the basis of bombardment or disease is unclear. However, it does seem difficult to imagine how anything other than deliberate murder can account for the small number of corpses with bullet holes in the head. Given the absence of German soldiers and the relative absence of Poles in the city, the Soviet Army seems the likely culprit for any such executions. This idea is supported by the failure of the Russians to release any archive material in their possession. The Katyn Wood massacre is a known Soviet atrocity and in all probability the mass graves at Malbork represent another of Stalin's crimes. The truth will almost certainly never be known.

WHO PLANTED THE BOMB AT THE WORLD'S FAIR?

On 4 July 1940, a time bomb exploded at the British Pavilion at the World's Fair in New York City. At that time the United States, in spite of the slight improvement in the economy as a result of the

New Deal, remained stubbornly stuck in recession, so the World's Fair was conceived by President Roosevelt as a symbolic gesture to raise morale and help lift America out of the Depression. Its theme was 'The Dawn of a New Day' and extensive redevelopment work took place in the Queens district of New York. A run-down area was transformed into a glittering showcase for displays from around 60 countries of the world.

The French Pavilion included a restaurant which proved so popular that it opened in Manhattan after the fair closed while the Soviet Union built a full-size replica of a train station on the Moscow Metro. The British Pavilion displayed the Crown jewels and the Magna Carta.

The fair opened in April 1939 and drew thousands of visitors. Although the outbreak of World War II in September 1939 cast a dark shadow over the upbeat attempts to lift spirits, the United States could at least congratulate itself that it was neutral in the conflict.

The opening ceremony, at which President Roosevelt and New York governor Herbert Lehman both made speeches, was broadcast live on television. Visitors gazed in wonder at such new inventions as air conditioning, the fax machine and an eight-foot-high robot. The fair's architecture was consciously futuristic and the whole event was described by the media as 'the eighth wonder of the world'.

The 'Avenue of Tomorrow' showed the latest Ford cars driving around the circuit. Salvador Dali contributed a typically bizarre installation called *The Dream of Venus*, featuring scantily clad women dressed as mermaids or even pianos. A time capsule created by the Westinghouse Corporation included such disparate elements as a packet of cigarettes and writings by Einstein.

Roosevelt's opening address struck a note of optimism and hope. He said:

The Americans offer up a silent prayer that on the continent of Europe, from which the American hemisphere was principally colonized, the years to come will break down many barriers to intercourse between nations.

Bomb explodes

All of this hope was brutally blown apart on 4 July 1940. The telephone operator at the British Pavilion received an anonymous call telling her to 'get out' as a bomb had been planted in the pavilion. Meanwhile, an electrician on the site discovered a suspicious-looking satchel and alerted security. It was removed to an area behind the Polish Pavilion.

Two police officers from the New York City Bomb Squad then arrived. The detectives, Joseph Lynch and Ferdinand Socha, heard the package ticking. Socha used a pocket knife to cut a hole in the case and Lynch peered through the gap and turned to his partner. 'It's the business,' he said.

Then the bomb exploded. Lynch and Socha took the full impact of the blast and were killed instantly, while four other police officers were seriously injured by the explosion.

Forensic analysis determined the bomb to be equal in force to the detonation of 12 sticks of dynamite. It created a hole in the floor three feet deep and five feet wide.

There was no shortage of suspects for the bombing. Top of the list were the Nazis and Nazi sympathizers and right-wing groups like the Christian Front were also questioned by the police. The IRA were considered potential culprits but were ruled out.

The most favoured group of suspects were the German American Bund. The first arrest of one of its members took place on 5 July 1940, following a raid on the Bund's offices. Several guns were discovered as well as maps of America with particular locations marked.

The police investigation failed to find any hard evidence against any group or individual. A large reward was offered for information about the bombing, but it produced no results and the crime remains unsolved.

This attack was not unusual in those days. On 11 September 1938, two bombs exploded in the fur district of New York and two weeks before the World's Fair bombing both the German Library of Information and the *Daily Worker* offices – a Communist newspaper – were bombed. There were over 400 bomb threats a week. Terrorism was rife and pro-Nazi groups, radical leftists and others attempted to push their agendas through violence.

Was it a British plot?

A conspiracy theory has been put forward by New York police officer Bernard Whalen. He suggests that the bomb was deliberately planted at the World's Fair by the British. Whalen points to Britain's isolation and Churchill's desperate attempts to persuade the Americans to enter the war. By contrast, Hitler had nothing to gain by committing a terrorist act that would increase the likelihood of US involvement. Whalen points out that 'one of the first things that came out of the bombing was anti-German sentiment'.

In support of his theory, Whalen says that Sir William Stephenson had been sent to New York City some weeks earlier to set up an MI6 operation. The bomb had been placed in an air conditioning unit which was not open to the public and an electrician had discovered the suspicious item and reported it. All of the security personnel in the British Pavilion were either current or former soldiers.

Whalen adds that there was a lack of co-operation between the British security staff and the police. He suggests that the FBI may have been involved in a cover-up because when he asked to see copies of their investigation into the attack he was told none existed. He believed that MI6 (and by implication some elements in the FBI) were complicit in planting a bomb to turn American public opinion against the Germans.

That is the nub of Whalen's case against British intelligence. It seems persuasive in many ways, but it is open to serious objections.

The most fundamental flaw in the theory is that it risked catastrophic failure. Churchill was half-American and was desperate to establish closer links with the United States, so it seems inconceivable that he would have authorized an operation of this kind. It is hardly more probable that Stephenson or the head of MI6 in Britain – whose authorization would surely have been necessary – would have countenanced such a risky move. The chances that 'rogue elements' within MI6 might have risked such an enterprise are equally dubious.

Whalen admits that what he saw as British officials impeding the investigation 'could just have been the stuffy British attitude'. It is equally possible that the FBI might have destroyed its records of the case or been unwilling to release them in case they revealed evidence of incompetence on their part.

Many pro-Nazis and radicals of far right and far left persuasions routinely used violence and terrorism. The IRA, for example, certainly bombed targets in Britain, was pro-Nazi and had many supporters in the United States. Conspiracy theories are always interesting, however, and the idea that MI6 planted the bomb in the British Pavilion is more plausible than most.

In spite of that, the most likely culprits are pro-Nazis in America or the IRA. Both had many mavericks among their members who were rash enough as well as callous enough to plant a bomb that could have killed hundreds of people. The case remains unsolved and will probably remain a baffling mystery.

TUNNEL OF DEATH

On 3 March 1944, the village of Balvano in the Apennine mountains of southern Italy was the scene of a horrific tragedy. Train No. 8017, 47 wagons long, left Salerno at 6 p.m. on 2 March 1944 and made its slow journey along the track. Theoretically it was purely a freight train but soldiers often rode on it, as well as hordes of black marketeers. That night it was carrying 800 passengers, most of them illegal boarders.

The final destination of the train should have been Potenza. At Romagnano it stopped to attach a second locomotive to the front of the vehicle to assist the underpowered and overcrowded train to climb the steep mountain route and continue its journey. It had only travelled 4 miles (6.5 km) before it was forced to stop once more because the train ahead of it had broken down and was blocking the line.

Forty-five minutes later Train 8017 was cleared to resume its journey. It was almost 1 a.m. and most of the passengers were asleep.

Only half a mile beyond the approaching Armi tunnel lay the village of Balvano. Trains stopped there to take on water and continue their laborious climb up into the mountains. When the train had left, the stationmaster telegraphed the next station on the line, Bella-Muro, to inform them of 8017's departure. He then returned to his cabin and relaxed, because it was an hour before the next train was due to arrive.

The journey to the next station should have taken 20 minutes. At first the Bella-Muro stationmaster simply assumed the train was running late. By contrast, the stationmaster at Balvano became increasingly concerned. When the next train arrived at 2.40 a.m., he detached the locomotive and ordered it to steam up the line to see if there had been an accident. The locomotive had barely left the station when an agitated man holding a red lantern shouted at him.

They're all dead!

As the stationmaster stepped off the footplate to greet him the man collapsed on the ground. In a barely audible voice he announced: 'They're all dead!' Taking the man back to the station, the stationmaster tried to discover what had happened.

The man was the brakeman on 8017 and he told the stationmaster how the train had come to a sudden, jolting halt when they were inside the tunnel. Only his brake van and three rear carriages had been outside the tunnel, while the remainder of the train was trapped inside. Walking along the track he entered the train and almost immediately saw bodies. He rushed out of the tunnel and began making his way towards Balvano, which was when he saw the stationmaster.

Hearing this tale, the stationmaster raced back to the tunnel and opened some of the carriage doors. Everyone appeared to be dead. Returning to his post, he raised the alarm at around 4 a.m.

American troops, Italian police and railway staff made their way to the stricken train.

They hooked up the brake van to a locomotive and hauled the train back to the station. Only then did the full extent of the disaster become apparent.

Hundreds of people lay dead. Out of 800 passengers, only five had survived and one of them died later. Those who had survived could give little insight into what had happened.

Following the grim salvage operation an investigation began into the cause of the disaster. The drivers and footplatemen were dead so they could not be interviewed. However, two of the surviving passengers believed that the train had slid backwards before shuddering to a sudden halt.

Railway accident investigators examined both locomotives and discovered that the controls on one had been set into reverse with the brakes off but the second one had its controls set for full steam ahead with its brakes full on. These conflicting courses of action by both drivers had paralysed the train.

Toxic gases and smoke from burning coal soon filled the tunnel. Mercifully, most of the passengers died in their sleep from inhaling the poisonous smoke.

An inquiry of sorts was held by the American military authorities and the disaster was declared to be 'an act of God'. The tragedy was hushed up but the Italian railway authorities then introduced new measures to help move trains through tunnels in order to prevent a similar incident occurring. There would be no more 'tunnels of death' on Italian railways, but these safety measures came too late for the hundreds who perished in this entirely avoidable tragedy.

CHAPTER FOUR

THE MAN WHO NEVER WAS

CHAPTER FOUR

Operation Mincemeat was the code name for the most successful disinformation project ever undertaken by the British. It deceived the Germans into believing that the Allies planned to invade Greece, the Balkans and Sardinia in 1943 rather than their real invasion target of Sicily.

The idea for Mincemeat originated on 29 September 1939 with a memo drafted by Ian Fleming, though under the signature of his superior officer. Fleming suggested planting false papers on a corpse that would be discovered by the enemy.

In 1942, the British tried out this ruse. Immediately prior to the Battle of Alam el Halfa, a dead body was placed in a scout car that was blown up. It contained a deliberately misleading map pretending to show the locations of British minefields. The Germans swallowed the trick and their tanks became trapped in the desert sand.

Charles Cholmondeley of MI5 and Ewan Montagu of naval intelligence resurrected Fleming's idea and began to examine ways of making it work. At the Casablanca Conference in January 1943, the Allies agreed to invade Sicily by July of that year but Churchill favoured deceiving the Germans about the target.

The plan was greatly assisted by Hitler's nervousness about the Balkans. The bulk of German oil and many other raw materials came from that region and if he lost control of those supplies his military position would be fatally weakened. British intelligence reinforced these fears by creating a fictitious army group in Cairo and conducting manoeuvres in Syria with dummy tanks. Everything possible was done to fool the Germans into expecting the main thrust of the invasion to be centred on Greece.

Montagu believed that Fleming's suggestion of planting false documents on a corpse could create additional ammunition for this deception. He therefore approached the leading pathologist,

Sir Bernard Spilsbury, for technical advice on how to 'plant' and prepare the corpse for discovery as well as information about the type of corpse that would be needed.

The original plan was to drop the body from an aircraft and pretend that the man had died in a plane crash. Spilsbury pointed out that victims of air crashes often died from shock so their lungs might not be full of water. He also stressed the Spanish dislike of post-mortems and the fact that the cause of death was not always obvious in an autopsy. Montagu, summarizing Spilsbury's findings, wrote:

British author and creator of James Bond, Ian Fleming worked for British naval intelligence during World War II.

If a post mortem examination was made by someone who had formed the preconceived idea that the death was probably due to drowning there was little likelihood that the difference between this liquid, in lungs that had started to decompose, and sea water would be noticed.

FINDING AND PREPARING THE CORPSE

It was clear that a relatively wide range of corpses could be used. Montagu set about finding a suitable body. He approached Bentley Purchase, the coroner for the northern district of London, who pointed out that 'even with bodies all over the place, each one has to be accounted for'.

On 28 January 1943 Purchase found a body that was suitable. He kept the unknown corpse in the mortuary fridge but stressed that it must be used within three months or the signs of decomposition would be obvious.

Montagu and Cholmondeley began developing the plan and it was approved by senior naval officers. They started to create a fictitious identity for the corpse, choosing to call him Captain (Acting Major) William Martin. He was described as a Royal Marine on attachment to Combined Operations Headquarters. The name was chosen because there were several serving marines called Martin and his assigned rank made him important enough to carry secret documents but not senior enough to be widely known.

An MI5 clerk called Jean Leslie posed as his fictitious fiancée Pam. Two 'love letters' were also written on her behalf. A fake receipt for a diamond engagement ring, letters from his 'father', a solicitor and a demand from the bank for payment of an overdraft were added to the fictitious dossier, to give 'Martin' greater credibility. Various other personal items were added to provide a complete fictitious itinerary for him from 18–24 April.

One problem was creating a photograph for his identity card. Attempts were made to take pictures of the corpse but it was impossible to disguise the fact that they were photographs of a dead body. Finally, an MI5 operative who resembled the corpse was found and his picture was used for 'Martin's' identity card.

The cards then needed to be given the appearance of age, so Montagu decided to rub them repeatedly on his trousers. Cholmondeley was approximately the same height and build, so he wore the corpse's uniform to create a 'lived in' impression. Once these problems had been resolved, it was necessary to decide on the contents of the false papers.

Montagu believed that it was essential for the documents to name Sicily, while making it clear that the island was a 'cover' for the real invasion site.

PLANTING THE BODY

After they had prepared the deception, Montagu and Cholmondeley considered the most practical method of 'planting' the corpse. They examined the west coast of Spain, Portugal and the south of France, but all were ruled out. In the end, Huelva on the southern coast of Spain was selected as 'Martin's' destination.

There were three points that made Huelva the final choice. One was that the tides and currents in the area made it more likely that the body would land where it needed to be found. Another was that, as Montagu wrote later: 'There was a very active German agent who had excellent contacts with certain Spaniards.' The third reason was that the British vice-consul was 'a reliable and helpful man'.

After considering aircraft drops and the use of ships, the decision was taken to use a submarine to dispose of the body in the desired location. 'Martin' was placed inside an airtight canister which was then filled with 21 lb (9.5 kg) of dry ice before being sealed up. By expelling the oxygen, this allowed the corpse to remain fresh without being refrigerated.

The submarine *Seraph* sailed on 19 April 1943 with its cargo, reaching the coast of Huelva on 29 April. Early next morning, it surfaced while the crew opened the canister and lowered the body into the sea.

Later that morning, the body was discovered by a Spanish fisherman. Soldiers were summoned and it was taken to Huelva. The British vice-consul reported to the Admiralty that the body of a British officer had been found with a briefcase. There followed various messages between the vice-consul and the Admiralty, all using a code which the British knew that the Germans had broken. These messages stressed how important it was for the vice-consul to recover the briefcase.

SWALLOWING THE BAIT

The following day two Spanish doctors performed an autopsy on the body in the presence of the vice-consul, who encouraged them to conclude proceedings quickly. They signed the death certificate for Major William Martin and recorded the cause of his death as drowning. Martin was buried with full military honours the following day.

The briefcase was held by the Spanish Navy, who refused to hand it over to the Germans, and on 5 May it was transferred to naval headquarters at San Fernando, where its contents were photographed. The letters had not been opened at this stage. Once the briefcase reached Madrid, a personal request was made to the

Spanish government by Admiral Canaris to allow the Germans to have the documents.

The Spanish removed the contents of the letters by winding the wet paper tightly across a probe and pulling it out of the envelopes gently. Then they dried and photographed the letters before soaking them in salt water and resealing them. On 8 May, the Germans received copies of all of the documents in the briefcase. An agent took them to Germany to deliver them personally.

On 11 May, everything was returned to the vice-consul. When the letters arrived in London British intelligence saw that they had been opened and read. Another cable, using the code which the Germans had already broken, was sent back to the vice-consul stating that nothing had been tampered with. He made sure that pro-Nazi Spaniards received this 'information'.

Then, on 14 May, the British intercepted a German communication warning that the main Allied invasion would take place in the Balkans. Montagu published 'Major Martin' in the list of British casualties in *The Times* for 4 June.

The same day saw Admiral Dönitz meet Hitler to discuss the situation. He declared:

> *The Führer does not agree that the most likely invasion point is Sicily. He believes that the discovered Anglo-Saxon order [the false documents in the briefcase] confirms the assumption that the attacks will be directed mainly against Sardinia and the Peloponnese.*

Hitler announced that Corsica, Sardinia and Greece would be defended 'at all costs'. He transferred a Panzer division to Salonika, doubled German troop strength in Sardinia and provided them with fighter aircraft as support. Two more Panzer divisions were moved from Russia to the Balkans and U-boats were relocated from Sicily to Greece. Seven German divisions were sent to Greece and a further ten to the Balkans.

On 9 July, the Allies invaded Sicily. Hitler continued to regard this as a diversionary bluff until almost the end of July and sent Rommel to Salonika to resist the expected main assault. Sicily fell within a month and the withdrawal of German troops from the Russian Front ensured Soviet victory in the Battle of Kursk. Operation Mincemeat had been a triumph of deception and the corpse had helped turn the tide of the war.

WHO WAS MAJOR MARTIN?

What is the true identity of 'Major William Martin', the 'Man Who Never Was?' There are at least three candidates, all of them plausible choices.

Former police officer Colin Gibson researched the case for 14 years and identified Martin as sailor Tom Martin from HMS *Dasher*. Then, in 2004, a memorial service was held on the current *Dasher*, at which another sailor on the ship, John Melville, was officially named as being Major Martin.

John Steele, another researcher, also believes that Melville was Martin. He says that 'Montagu pinched a body' and that 'the body used was from *Dasher*. And we couldn't have the British public finding out that a body was stolen.'

The third candidate is the Welsh tramp Glyndwr Michael. Denis Smyth, another researcher into Mincemeat, is convinced that Michael's body was used in the deception. There are two main pieces of evidence that support his theory and both come from Montagu.

One is a 'most secret' memo from Montagu reporting a conversation between himself and coroner Bentley Purchase. He wrote:

Adolf Hitler with Admiral Dönitz at the Wolf's Lair, the Eastern Front military HQ, in 1942.

Mincemeat took a minimal dose of a rat poison containing phosphorus. This dose was not sufficient to kill him outright and its only effect was to so impair the functioning of the liver that he died a little time afterwards.

Smyth points out that Montagu is discussing whether the traces of rat poison could be detected by Spanish doctors in an autopsy. He says: 'The person buried in Spain died from taking rat poison, not drowning, and therefore it is Glyndwr Michael.'

Another point in favour of the theory is that Montagu described the corpse as being that of 'a ne'er do well' and 'the only worthwhile thing that he ever did he did after his death'. It is surely more probable that he would have used those words about Michael, an alcoholic tramp, rather than a sailor from the *Dasher* who had died in an explosion.

Montagu also said to Purchase that the corpse did not look like a fit officer, to which the coroner retorted that 'he does not have to look like an officer – only a staff officer'.

Steele, Gibson and Smyth remain convinced that their candidates are the true 'Man Who Never Was'. However, Bill Jewell, commander of the *Seraph* submarine, described it as being 'highly unlikely' that the body of a tramp would have been used.

On balance, particularly in the light of Montagu's comments, Michael is perhaps the most likely candidate for 'Major Martin'. Whoever he was, his true identity remains uncertain and will probably always be one of the great unsolved wartime mysteries.

CHAPTER FIVE
LOST TREASURES

THE AMBER ROOM

The Amber Room was a spectacular chamber created as part of the Charlottenburg Palace in Berlin. It was designed in the baroque style in the early 18th century and remained in Berlin until 1716, when Frederick William I of Prussia presented it to his ally Peter the Great of Russia. Peter moved it to the Catherine Palace near St Petersburg and expanded the room. When it was completed, it occupied 590 ft^2 (55 m^2) and contained 13,000 lb (5,900 kg) of amber.

When the Germans invaded the Soviet Union the curators tried to hide it behind wallpaper. This disguise failed, however, and German Army Group North disassembled the entire room, a task that took them 36 hours.

By 14 October 1941, it had been transferred to the castle of Königsberg in Germany (now Kalingrad, Russia).

In August 1944, the city was extensively firebombed by the RAF and, in January 1945, Hitler ordered all looted valuables to be removed. Albert Speer attempted to carry out this command, but was hampered by the flight of the governor, Erich Koch. The remnants of the German Army took command and assisted Speer in removing the stolen artefacts, then in April 1945 the Red Army pounded Königsberg with heavy artillery and inflicted further damage before its final capture on 9 April.

Following the Russian occupation of the city the Amber Room disappeared. Various reports of its sighting followed, though none were ever confirmed. However, a number of eyewitnesses stated that they had seen the room being loaded on to the *Wilhelm Gustloff* ship, which departed from Gotenhafen (now Gdynia) on 30 January 1945, but was sunk by a Russian submarine. According to this account, the room sank to the bottom of the ocean along with the vessel.

But then came the first concrete evidence that at least a fragment of the room had survived. In 1997, an Italian stone mosaic that had once been part of a set of stones decorating the room was discovered in Germany. It belonged to the family of a soldier who had helped to pack the room before it was moved (and had presumably looted part of the consignment himself). The mosaic was returned to the Russians and used in their attempt to reconstruct the Amber Room.

Then in 1998 two teams claimed to have found the whereabouts of the Amber Room. A Lithuanian team declared that it was buried in a lagoon while a German team stated that it was buried in a silver mine. Neither claim survived further investigation.

In 2004, two British researchers, after a lengthy study of Soviet archives, came to the conclusion that the room had been destroyed during the Russian assault on Königsberg. They cite the testimony of Alexander Brusov, who was in charge of the Russian team tasked

The Amber Room, a full-size chamber styled in ornate baroque and rococo designs, given by William I of Prussia to Peter the Great in the early 18th century.

with recovering the Amber Room at the end of the war. Brusov's report declared: 'Summarizing all the facts, we can say that the Amber Room was destroyed between 9 and 11 April 1945.' Some years later, Brusov claimed that it had not been destroyed but instead it had survived and had been removed by the Germans.

The Soviet report declared that most of the Italian mosaics had been retrieved from the ruins of Königsberg castle. There is no doubt that the Russians invested considerable time and effort in the search for the Amber Room.

The only possible conclusions are that the Amber Room was either destroyed by the aerial and artillery bombardment or that somehow it was successfully removed from Königsberg. Some contemporary residents of the city claim that parts of the room were discovered by the Red Army in the castle's cellars and that they transported these remains to a nearby storehouse. Unfortunately, though, the extraordinary decision in 1968 by the Soviet leader Leonid Brezhnev to destroy the castle means that archaeological research on the site is almost impossible.

Survival theories

A new claim to have identified the Amber Room's resting place was made in October 2017. Three German researchers examined reports from the KGB and the Stasi and then used radar equipment to detect anything that might lie beneath 'the Prince's Cave' near Hartenstein. One of the researchers told *The Times* that they found 'a very big, deep and long tunnel system and we detected something that we think could be a booby trap'.

Witnesses testify that a large number of crates were stored inside the tunnels before the entrances were blown up to conceal them. The three men want to excavate the site but 'need a sponsor', as one of them told journalists.

Another group of people suggested that the location for the Amber Room is the city of Wuppertal. Karl-Heinz Kleine and his bowling club claim that it was transported from Königsberg in early 1945. Kleine said:

> *Erich Koch, the Nazi Gauleiter of East Prussia who died in a Polish prison in 1986, came from Wuppertal. As the Red Army closed in on Königsberg, he ordered the treasure to be packed up and brought back to his homeland.*

He points out that the city is honeycombed with underground tunnels and bunkers dug by the Nazis. Kleine believes that somewhere in this subterranean morass lie the crates containing the lost Amber Room.

Another candidate for its final resting place is Lake Toplitz, situated in a dense forest in the Austrian Alps. Norman Scott was told by an eyewitness that in April 1945 he saw exactly 27 crates being dropped into the waters of the lake. According to the records of the Reich Main Security Office of the SS, the Amber Room was packed into 27 crates before being removed. An American expedition to the lake in 2006 spent £7 million on their investigations, but found little beyond a crate with Cyrillic lettering. So far, Lake Toplitz has yielded nothing more concrete than millions of pounds' worth of forged British banknotes.

A further theory is that the room is hidden within disused mine shafts in an East German forest. This location, Poppen Wood, has inspired hordes of treasure hunters to descend on the site, but to date nothing resembling the Amber Room has been discovered.

Whether the Amber Room was destroyed during an RAF raid in 1944, during the Russian bombardment in 1945 or was spirited away to a secret location remains an unanswered question. No one knows the fate of this lost masterpiece of baroque design. It may remain an unsolved mystery until the end of time.

THE MYSTERY OF HITLER'S MISSING GLOBE

Hitler's globe was immortalized in Charlie Chaplin's satirical parody *The Great Dictator*. Chaplin portrays the globe as a type of balloon or beach ball that bursts in Hitler's face.

The real object was called the Columbus Globe for State and Industry Leaders and it was made in Berlin during the 1930s. There were two limited editions of the globe. One was made for the Nazi Party and the other was for Hitler. Hitler's globe was almost as large as a Volkswagen car and cost more to produce, while the globe for the Nazi Party was made out of wood and lacked the individual features of what was nicknamed 'the Führer globe'.

It is unclear how many copies of the globe were produced as the factory which made them was destroyed in an air raid in 1943, along with its records. There cannot have been large numbers of these collectable items but there are certainly rival claimants to the title of 'the Führer globe'. Three sites in Berlin possess what each believes to be the 'real' Hitler globe. The most widely accepted claim is that of the German Historical Museum, though the Märkisches Museum and a geographical institute in the city also believe that theirs is the genuine Hitler globe, satirized by Chaplin. Two sites in Munich also claim to house 'the Führer globe'. In spite of their claims, photographic evidence demonstrates that none of them are the globe that once stood in the Reich Chancellery office – the 'Hitler globe'.

Wolfram Pobanz, a cartographer, has devoted 40 years to studying the various Hitler globes and has established the provenance of all of the examples in the public domain. The globe in the German Historical Museum, for instance, is identical to a drawing made by the architect Paul Ludwig Troost for Ribbentrop's foreign ministry. As Pobanz says: 'This globe could only have been made for Ribbentrop.'

One globe turned up for auction in 2007 and was sold for $100,000. It was looted from Berchtesgaden by the American soldier John Barsamian on 10 May 1945. Barsamian's globe sits on a wooden base with a metal half-meridian at the north and south poles. It is 18 in (45 cm) high and has a diameter of 12 in (30 cm). All of the markings on the globe are in German and they show the borders of Germany as they existed in late 1939.

Pobanz admits that Barsamian's object was a Columbus globe, but denies that it is 'the' Hitler globe. His researches have led him to make contact with globe enthusiasts across the world and he believes that several surviving examples are in private collections.

The curator of the German Historical Museum describes Pobanz as 'a very serious man with a passion for this type of globe'. Pobanz declares that none of the globes in private hands are the 'true' Hitler globe. Ironically, he believes:

> Hitler probably didn't think anything about the globe. There's no picture of him standing beside the globe. If the globe had actually meant anything special to Hitler, there would surely be a photograph.

Lavrenti Beria was the first senior Soviet official to view the Reich Chancellery after the capture of Berlin and it has been suggested that he took the globe with him to the NKVD (later KGB and now FSB) headquarters in Lubianka. Enquiries from both the KGB and its successor the FSB have proved fruitless, with the ministries refusing either to confirm or deny the story.

Pobanz wonders if the real Hitler globe may have been looted by the Russians. He gives as evidence a photograph of a group of Soviet soldiers occupying the Reich Chancellery in May 1945. They are gathered around Hitler's globe. 'Maybe it's in Moscow,' Pobanz suggests. 'I don't know where it is.'

THE MISSING NAZI 'BLOOD FLAG'

The *Blutfahne* – the 'blood flag' – was the flag carried during the unsuccessful Munich putsch in 1923, when it became soaked with the blood of a fallen Nazi. It was one of the most venerated Nazi relics and it was not only displayed at every important Nazi event but it was also used to touch other Nazi flags in a kind of 'blessing' ritual. Another purpose of the flag was to 'seal' the oath of new SS recruits.

The *Blutfahne* was kept on display in the Brown House (Nazi HQ) in Munich except when it was brought out for ceremonial purposes. However, an air raid on Munich in January 1945 scored a direct hit on the building and it is possible that the flag was destroyed during the bombing.

Another possibility is that as Allied troops approached Munich the SS began destroying incriminating records. It is highly unlikely that the Nazis would have destroyed one of their most 'sacred' relics but they may have tried to hide it under the debris of the bombed building. In 1946 and 1947 Allied troops sifted through the debris in search of evidence. There is nothing in their records to suggest that they found the *Blutfahne*, which suggests that they were unable to locate it.

In 1947, they blew up the Honour temples at the front of the Brown House and the debris from their excavations and the demolition work was removed and dumped on the present site of the Olympiapark.

Some sources claim that the *Blutfahne* was taken out of the Brown House in late 1944 and moved to another site in Munich and that in spring 1945 it was moved once more, this time to an unknown location.

The Allies were certainly anxious to recover the flag. Its standard bearer, Jakob Grimminger, was extensively grilled by the Americans but denied all knowledge of its whereabouts. If he did know its hidden destination then Grimminger took his secret with him to the grave.

In the 1980s an article appeared in the Chilean newspaper *El Mercurio*. It claimed that the *Blutfahne* was now deposited in a bank in Santiago but no details were given of how it had arrived there or who had deposited the relic.

The idea that a U-boat smuggled it to safety in South America has also become popular. Some versions of this story even suggest that Bormann took it to his secret lair in Paraguay.

A former SS officer is alleged to have told a blogger that the flag is safely concealed in a secret location in Germany or Austria. The same blogger spoke to a former Hitler Youth member and was informed that an 'Old Fighter' – a Nazi who was with Hitler in the days before he came to power – had said that it was safe in Europe and was being guarded by other Nazis.

Third Reich memorabilia are highly prized and many private collectors have tried to track down the *Blutfahne* but without success. It would command a high price if it was ever made available for public auction.

Grimminger was chosen by Hitler to be the sole custodian of the flag. It remains uncertain whether he knew more than he admitted and was well aware of its hidden location or whether he was overcome by the chaos and turmoil of the last days of the Reich and had no idea what had happened to the flag.

Lost, destroyed or concealed, the mystery of its present whereabouts remains unsolved.

WHERE IS ROMMEL'S GOLD?

'Rommel's gold' is the nickname given to the treasure looted from the Jewish community in Tunisia during the German occupation of North Africa. A more accurate name for it would be 'Rauff's gold' as Rommel had nothing to do with either its acquisition or its removal.

SS colonel Walter Rauff slaughtered and pillaged the Jews he found in Tunisia and at least 2,500 of them died at his hands. Gold, diamonds, precious gems and other valuable items were stolen from the victims, with most of his plunder being taken in a single day.

In January 1943, Rauff went with two lorries carrying armed SS men to the town of Gabes in Tunisia. He ordered the rabbi to summon all the leaders of the Jewish community to hear his proposal.

A hundred Jews – rabbis, traders, businessmen and other important community figures – went to meet him. Rauff offered them a choice.

'*Sie könnten sich mit sechzig Zentnorn gold freikaufen,*' he said. 'For sixty hundredweight of gold you can remain free.'

The unspoken words 'and alive' were surely on the minds of his listeners. They knew that Rauff had already murdered and plundered other North African Jews. He gave them a deadline of 48 hours to bring him the gold and as he spoke he pointed to the armed men behind him. There was no mistaking what the consequences would be in the event of non-compliance.

However, it was accomplished and two days later Rauff and his armed escort left, laden with six chests of gold and treasure. The value of this hoard has never been established.

Three days later Rauff's convoy arrived at the port of Sfax, where a ship was loaded with the containers. It sailed from the

Quai de Commerce and its destination was Italy, the first stop on its intended journey to Germany.

Rauff's cargo sailed safely to Naples, where it was then handed over into the custody of four German officers. Their orders were to transport it by land across Italy and through Austria into Germany. Allied air raids on Italy and the growing unpopularity of Mussolini made that a risky venture so once the convoy reached Rome they were ordered to ferry the cases by sea to Corsica. Once the convoy was safely on the island, it would travel to the port of La Spezia before resuming its overland path into Germany.

A mysterious expedition to Corsica followed on 16 September 1943. The four officers summoned a diver called Peter Fleig to meet them at Bastia. He was put into a diving suit and taken on a motorboat to locate 'a particularly unusual rock formation'. When he found it underwater, he returned and its co-ordinates were marked on a chart.

He was taken back to Bastia and saw 'six lead and tin crates of valuables. They were full of jars of gold, silver chalices, little

Former SS Obersturmbannführer Walter Rauff after his arrest in Punta Arenas, Chile, in 1962.

religious caskets set with precious stones, diamonds, jewellery, pearls and a number of paintings.'

On 18 September, the four German officers decided that heavy Allied bombing and the instability in Italy made it too dangerous to try and take the treasure overland. Instead, Fleig was ordered to dive with the crates to the previously recorded position and mark the spot where they had been deposited with four weighted buoys. It took 30 ft (9 m) of cable to secure them.

Later that afternoon, Fleig and the four officers arrived at La Spezia, where the senior member of the party reported his actions to the German commandant. All five were arrested and although Fleig was beaten by the SS and imprisoned for a month he was eventually released. The four officers, on the other hand, were court-martialled and shot.

Searching for treasure

After the war, Fleig intended to return to Corsica. He had made a careful note of the position of the chests and was determined to claim the treasure for himself. After approaching the French authorities, he made the first of many dives in search of the lost riches. He was personally involved in several of them, though none successfully located any evidence of the stolen treasure.

In 2006, a German TV company sent divers to Corsica with sonar equipment to help them detect any treasure. This was an unauthorized expedition and the French government fined them and sent them away. Nevertheless, their explorations uncovered nothing.

Then in 2007, a British researcher, Terry Hodgkinson, announced plans to search for the missing loot. He declared: 'We are confident of the location. The treasure apparently lies in waters less than a nautical mile off Bastia.'

The value of the lost treasure is estimated to be at least £250 million.

Ian Fleming discovered the story of 'Rommel's gold' while he was working for British intelligence when a commando raid on Tambach castle in Bavaria unearthed German naval archives. It was while studying this material that Fleming learned about the stolen gold.

He tried to persuade the *Sunday Times* to finance an expedition to recover the treasure, but the cost was prohibitive and they refused. Instead, he wrote a fictionalized account of the story in his novel *On Her Majesty's Secret Service*.

Whatever the true fate of 'Rommel's gold' may be, its present whereabouts remain unknown. Even if one day it was recovered, it would be tainted treasure, blood money surrendered at the point of a gun to avoid genocide.

THE NAZI GOLD TRAIN

There are several stories about a train carrying vast quantities of gold and treasure being buried in an underground tunnel in 1945. It is said to lie in Lower Silesia, near the city of Waldenburg (now Walbrzych). A train supposedly left Breslau (now Wroclaw) and was driven underground into the tunnels beneath the Owl mountains. On its arrival, it was buried within the vast network of tunnels and mines.

According to the stories gold, precious gems, stolen artwork and weapons were concealed in this underground hiding place. Various attempts have been made to locate it, but none have been successful and many historians now doubt if the train ever existed.

August 2015 saw a renewed flurry of interest when the German Andreas Richter and the Pole Piotr Koper, later revealed as mine owners, claimed to have heard a death-bed confession about the location of the train. They received permission from the Polish government to begin exploration of the area known as 'Zone 65'.

Richter and Koper claimed that radar images showed the presence of a large train. The governor of the region was more sceptical and remarked: 'There is no more proof for this alleged discovery than for other claims made over the years.'

On 4 September 2015, Richter and Koper released a statement in which they announced that they knew the precise location of the train. They also released photographs that seemed to show a deep shaft with some kind of object within. The two men claimed that the train's hidden resting place was on a stretch of track between Wroclaw and Walbrzych.

First of all, the Polish government fenced off woodland, removed trees and looked for possible bombs and mines. Once the military authorities had confirmed their absence, the men were given permission to conduct their search.

By November 2015, two teams had begun working on the site. One was headed by Richter and Koper and the other by the Kraków Mining Academy. The Academy team declared on 15 December that no evidence of any train had been discovered, though it was possible that the site contained a collapsed tunnel. Richter and Koper refused to accept this assessment.

In August 2016, they began excavating, employing a team of 64 people. The excavation cost $131,000 (£100,000). After seven days of intensive digging, the search was abandoned. Not a trace was found of train, tracks, tunnel or treasure. The radar images on which Richter and Koper had placed so much emphasis were revealed as being natural formations in the ice.

In spite of their abject failure, the two men announced that they would continue their search for the lost train in nearby locations. For the moment, all that can be said with certainty is that no missing train or treasure has ever been discovered. Whether it will be found at some time in the future or whether the whole story is simply a legend may never be known. For the present, the mystery of the Nazi 'gold train' remains an unsolved puzzle.

THE MYSTERY OF THE LOOTED NAZI TREASURES

Besides the loot stolen from the Jewish community in Tunisia, there was systematic looting of financial, artistic and other treasures from countries occupied by the Nazis. The whereabouts of much of this loot remains unknown. Even more controversial is the fate of the Reichsbank treasures.

The true extent of the gold, silver, artwork and other treasures stolen by the Nazis will probably never be known. However, the World Jewish Congress claims that gold and other items stolen from Jews by Nazis – including gold fillings from the teeth of Holocaust victims – are illegally held by the Bank of England and the Federal Reserve Bank in New York. It claims that much of this plunder is held by or laundered through Swiss banks.

There is no doubt that Switzerland colluded with the Nazis and that Swiss banks benefited to an unknown extent from the looted money and treasures stored in them. Eventually, they were compelled to pay $1.25 billion (£960,000,000) in compensation, but the true extent of their corrupt dealings has never been established.

Other sources, including American intelligence agencies, claim that the Vatican holds Nazi gold to the value of 350 million Swiss francs ($350 million/£266 million). This gold is said to be held in the vaults of the Vatican Bank and primarily consists of gold coins. The Vatican denies this claim but has refused to allow access to its archives for independent verification.

Another theory is that gangster Meyer Lansky, known as the 'Mob's Accountant', went to Switzerland and transferred some

$300 million into Swiss accounts. This was then further laundered until it came back as 'clean' money into the hands of the US Mafia.

There is no doubt that at the end of the war both American and Soviet troops looted much of the stolen plunder, either as individuals or on behalf of their governments. Some soldiers became rich as a result of stealing treasures, though mainly it was governments who prospered. Many Germans, both soldiers and civilians, also stole from the secret caches of money and other assets which had been concealed in the last stages of the war.

Allies discover Reichsbank cache

One of the most controversial aspects of Nazi loot is the story of the lost Reichsbank deposits. The Reichsbank contained huge gold reserves, which from 1938 onwards were extensively added to by plunder from Austria, Czechoslovakia, Holland, Hungary, Albania, France, Belgium and the Soviet Union. And during their retreat from Italy, the Nazis looted $100 million worth of Italian gold. The bank also held currency, stocks and shares and jewellery, much of it looted from concentration camp inmates.

The deputy director of the bank, Emil Puhl, was also a director of a Swiss bank. He used this channel to dispose of much of the loot from the victims of genocide.

On 3 February 1945, the Reichsbank was hit in a heavy bombing raid. The building was virtually destroyed and it became necessary to remove its holdings to a place of greater safety. The decision was taken to ship the gold and currency reserves to a potassium mine at Merkers in Thuringia.

On 9 February, the currency holdings of the bank were transferred to Merkers. Three days later, most of the gold was also dispatched. By 18 February, the bank's holdings were lodged in the Thuringian mine.

When the Americans crossed the Rhine on 22 March, frantic attempts were made to move the treasure from Merkers. Some of the currency was successfully moved, but the task of moving the gold was too difficult.

On 4 April 1945, American forces captured Merkers and by 7 April they discovered the mine and began exploring it. They found nearly a billion Reichsmarks in currency. An inner section of the mine then had to be dynamited and its opening up led to an astonishing treasure hoard.

Gold bars, gold coins, more currency, gold and silver plate, gold from teeth, jewellery and miscellaneous items were discovered. They also recovered paintings, sculptures and other artworks.

So important was this cache of treasures that Generals Bradley, Eisenhower and Patton came to inspect it themselves. Eisenhower decided to move it to the Reichsbank building in Frankfurt and, on 14 April, the mine's treasures were removed. Then on 15 April, they were transferred to their new home in Frankfurt.

Nazis move remaining reserves

News that the Reichsbank reserves at Merkers had been captured by the Americans shocked the Nazi leaders. Walther Funk, the bank president, pleaded with Hitler to move the remaining reserves out of Berlin. Russian troops were advancing steadily and there was no time to be lost if the remaining assets were to be saved.

The task of moving the holdings was placed in the hands of Friedrich Rauch, a senior police officer. It took his team between 4 and 13 April to collect most of the reserves from those German banks not already under Allied occupation. Banknotes were sent by train and gold by road. The railway transit was a nightmare and the paper currency took two weeks to reach its destination in Munich. However, the road convoy made better time and by

19 April, all of the holdings were transferred from Munich to Peissenberg, 80 miles (129 km) south of the city.

The plan was to stow the treasure in a lead mine but it was waterlogged. This resulted in a call to Funk who asked for the currency to be returned to Munich. The rest of the reserves he suggested should be entrusted to Colonel Franz Pfeiffer, an officer at the local Mountain Infantry Training School.

On 21 April, the banknotes were returned to Munich while the rest of the cargo headed south. Next day, Hitler finally admitted that the war was lost. Himmler ordered SS General Berger to hide the foreign currency held by the Reichsbank, but Berger stole the money instead and concealed it under the floorboards of a barn belonging to a forester. On his capture, Berger surrendered some of the money he had stolen but most of it was never recovered.

Minister of the Economy Walther Funk rolls up for the opening of the annual spring fair at the Gewandhaus, 1938.

By now law and order had broken down in Germany. An SS group went to the new Berlin headquarters of the Reichsbank and simply stole whatever they could find. They held up the staff at gunpoint and removed over $9 million worth of foreign exchange. The loot was transferred to Burgwies in Austria. On its arrival there, the SS discovered that Allied troops were so close that moving the treasure was out of the question, so they hastily buried their stolen goods under trees.

Other treasures were gradually distributed among other SS men and then the notorious Lieutenant Colonel Otto Skorzeny arrived. He took the loot up to the mountainside and buried it. None of the treasure buried by Skorzeny has ever been found. As he became a wealthy man after the war, there is little doubt that Skorzeny returned to the place where he had hidden the treasure and simply stole it to enrich himself.

The SS had stolen vast quantities of money, gold and jewels. Following their departure the Red Army arrived in Berlin. On 15 May, the Reichsbank was ordered to open its vaults and safes. Shortly afterwards its contents – valued at over $400 million in notes, coins, gold bars and bonds – were simply taken away by the Russians and never seen again.

Whether the major in charge of the operation pocketed the treasure himself or handed it over to the Soviet government has never been established.

The fate of the treasure buried at Mittenwald by Franz Pfeiffer remains controversial. He and his men unloaded the contents of the trucks at night, aware that American forces were not far away. It was discovered that one bag of gold bars had already gone missing and in spite of frantic searches it could not be located. Clearly it had been stolen but there was no time to make further investigations into its fate.

Concealing the Nazi treasure

Faced with the ever-advancing Americans, Pfeiffer spoke to local foresters, asking them for advice on the best sites to conceal the treasure. A portion of it was stored in a forester's house. It took days for the shipment to be moved. Then some of the banknotes and printing plates were taken on a boat to the Walchensee and sunk.

On 30 April, the Americans captured the area. Pfeiffer attempted to surrender to them but was told to wait until the morning. He and Rauch then dressed themselves as forest rangers and went into hiding.

Funk was captured by the Americans on 6 May. A team known as the Allied Monuments, Fine Arts and Archaeology Sub-Commission then began searching for the treasure looted by the Nazis. An additional group, known as the 'Gold Rush' team, tried to locate any money, gold and other valuables that had not already been discovered in the Merkers mine.

Everything that was unearthed was shipped to Frankfurt and stored in its Reichsbank building, but small thefts took place even while it was being deposited. It was obvious that the security at the building was not as rigorous as it should have been. The material stored there was not even formally inventoried.

Lieutenant Herbert DuBois was put in charge of tracking down the gold buried by Pfeiffer. Little is known of this officer and even his nationality is disputed. He may have been French or American and he spoke fluent German. DuBois sent soldiers out to search for the gold and interrogated a number of German prisoners for around a week, eventually producing an incomplete report. Another officer replaced him and was more thorough in his investigations.

One of the captives mentioned Pfeiffer's name and the investigators began to track him down. He had gone to ground and had spent some time sleeping rough before he made contact with Gebhart von Blücher, a descendant of the famous Blücher who had fought alongside Wellington at Waterloo.

Blücher and his family took Pfeiffer in. He asked the family to help him hide what he referred to as 'vast sums of foreign currency and gold'. A plan to ship it to the Vatican was discussed, but in the short term it was decided simply to conceal the treasure in a secure location.

Every night Pfeiffer and Rauch walked to the Walchensee, climbed the Klausenkopf and loaded two rucksacks each with dollars and pounds in banknotes. Millions of dollars' worth of notes were also brought into the Blücher house and then repacked into jars, jugs, pots and similar containers before being buried in the garden. After a while, it became necessary to find other hiding places. A number of log cabins in the Loisach Valley were used to bury around another $5 million in notes.

Who took the Nazi gold?

The US Army continued its search for the gold and arrested more people. This time some of them knew at least a few of the details of the burial places of the treasure. An intensive search was now undertaken.

On 7 June, after one of the Germans who had been involved with the disposal of the treasure cracked under sustained interrogation, a group of American soldiers finally reached the Steinriegel mountain. There, among a clump of trees, they found the first cache of gold. The eventual haul was 364 bags of gold including 728 gold bullion bars worth $10 million. This consignment was eventually transferred to the Reichsbank building in Frankfurt.

A couple of weeks later a further cache of gold was discovered in a bunker on the side of a mountain near Krün, to the north-east of

Mittenwald. The officer in charge of digging it up and transporting it said that it 'was stacked about 3 feet high, 3 feet square, in I would say about four stacks'. His troops loaded the gold on to two trucks with two drivers and two intelligence officers. He added: 'Then they drove away and I never saw them or the gold again.' It vanished from the record – in spite of attempts to cover up its loss and pretend that it was the same cache of gold discovered on 7 June – and was almost certainly stolen. Who was responsible for its theft remains unclear. It may have been private acquisitiveness by the soldiers or intelligence officers or it may have been simply transferred secretly to American custody with no record of it being entered into the inventory.

Whatever the truth, a huge quantity of gold vanished from sight and its whereabouts remains unknown. Germans, Russians and Americans were all involved in stealing some of the treasure. The story of the wholesale theft of millions in banknotes, securities and gold has aptly been called 'the greatest robbery in history'.

HOW DID CORNELIUS GURLITT ACQUIRE HIS ART COLLECTION?

In 2012, around 1,500 priceless works of art were discovered in the homes of Cornelius Gurlitt at Munich and Salzburg. They included paintings by Paul Cézanne, Claude Monet, Gustave Courbet, Ernst Ludwig Kirchner and Otto Dix. Gurlitt inherited the collection from his father Hildebrand Gurlitt, who had been given the task of acting as an art dealer on behalf of Hitler.

In November 2017, the Kunstmuseum Bern and the Bundeskunsthalle in Bonn held a joint exhibition of the collection. There are legal disputes over its proper ownership and the treasure trove of lost art has been described as 'spectacular'.

Before the Nazis came to power Hildebrand Gurlitt was a museum director in Zwickau. He championed modern art throughout the 1920s, but with growing support for the Nazis and their ideological hostility towards modernism he was dismissed from his post.

In 1933, he became director of a gallery in Hamburg but was dismissed for refusing to raise the swastika flag. He then became an art dealer with his own gallery, but because of his Jewish ancestry (he was a quarter Jewish) he was forced to register it in his wife's name.

Frustrated by his inability to make progress, Gurlitt began to collaborate with the Nazis. He wrote to Goebbels' propaganda ministry and offered his services as one of the leading experts in modern art. The ministry chose him as one of four dealers who would act on behalf of the Nazis by acquiring works of art for the Führermuseum project in Linz.

Following the defeat of Germany he was questioned by Allied specialists about missing art but was able to convince them that his role had been a minor one and he had not dealt with any works of value. He then became the director of an art gallery in Düsseldorf and died peacefully in 1961.

His son Cornelius inherited his father's secret cache and made periodic trips across the border into Switzerland, where he sold pieces from his father's art collection. In 2010 he was arrested by a customs officer in Germany on his return from Switzerland. The customs officer discovered around €9,000 ($10,000/£7,800) on him. It was not a large sum, but it still aroused suspicion. In fact, Gurlitt was in the habit of depositing the proceeds of his art sales in Switzerland and withdrawing €9,000 every month or so to cover his living expenses. This led to a full investigation into his activities by the tax authorities, who located and confiscated his hoard.

Ownership disputes

The following year he died and left his collection to the Bern Museum. This led to a legal dispute over the status and provenance of the artworks in question. Nevertheless, five of the works he owned have been returned to their former owners – Henri Matisse's *Seated Woman*, Adolf von Menzel's *Interior of a Gothic Church*, Camille Pissarro's *The Seine and the Louvre* and Max Liebermann's *Riders on the Beach*. Works by Renoir, Rodin, Signac and Munch are currently having their provenance investigated with a view to their possible return to their former owners.

Cézanne's *Montagne Sainte Victoire* was discovered behind a cupboard in Gurlitt's home in Salzburg. The Cézanne family is engaged in a legal dispute and wishes it to be returned to them.

Many of these works of art were confiscated from public galleries under the Nazis on the grounds that they were 'degenerate art'. Others were looted or bought at peppercorn prices from their Jewish owners. Following the Nazi conquest of most of Europe, wholesale looting occurred and many of Gurlitt's pieces may have been acquired in their wake.

The Nazis both collected works of art for the private collections of Goering and Hitler and sold them abroad to raise foreign currency. However, millions of pounds' worth of artwork have been lost for good and the Gurlitt collection is perhaps the largest cache of stolen art ever discovered.

The truth about how much of it Hildebrand Gurlitt acquired through theft and how much by holding back on some of his treasures will never be known. Nor will we ever discover how much has been destroyed or is lost for ever. It all represents a sad chapter in the history of art and one that remains unsolved.

CHAPTER SIX

SCIENTIFIC MYSTERIES

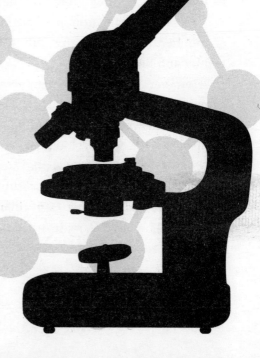

HANS COLER'S FREE ENERGY MACHINE

One of the most intriguing scientific mysteries of World War II is the 'free energy machine' designed by Hans Coler. We are extremely fortunate to have a record of this device, including detailed drawings, an account of its operation and extensive test results. After the war ended, British intelligence agents debriefed Coler extensively. In addition to the interviews with him, his machine was tested by British and foreign scientists. To their surprise and puzzlement, it worked perfectly.

Coler began working on 'an apparatus for generating electrical energy' as early as 1923. He spent three years experimenting with a device which was examined by a number of scientists and engineers. They observed, with considerable astonishment, that Coler's invention produced 'an energy surplus or energy multiplication', but they were unable to understand how and why it did so. Coler had no idea why his device worked either, but there is no doubt that it did.

On the strength of these assessments, he applied for a patent in 1925 but was turned down on the grounds that his invention was a 'perpetual motion machine'. He then temporarily abandoned his project after failing to find funding for further testing and development.

However, in 1933 the new Nazi government was more sympathetic towards unorthodox scientific ideas. Coler was able to resume his project with funding and research facilities made available for further development.

Coler's first device was the *Magnetstromapparat* developed in 1933, initially with the assistance of Willi von Unruh. They were later joined by Franz Haid of Siemens-Schukert. Haid built a model following Coler's instructions in December 1933, which worked successfully. Other models were then made and examined by two scientists, both of whom confirmed that they worked. One example of Coler's device was locked in a room for three months and still continued to function.

Coler's *Magnetstromapparat* consisted of six magnets coiled in such a way that the circuit included both the magnets and the winding coil. They were arranged in a hexagon and connected to a circuit including two condensers, a switch and two solenoidal coils, one sliding inside the other. The switch was left open and the magnets separated slightly. The sliding coil was then adjusted until a signal appeared on the voltmeter, after which the switch was closed. Gradually the power built up to a maximum level of 12 watts.

Neither Coler nor any of the other scientists and engineers who tested the device could explain how and why it worked. After a while, Coler began to evolve some theories. None were in accordance with orthodox scientific theories on electromagnetism, the laws of motion or the laws of thermodynamics.

The *Stromerzeuger* was the second device invented by Coler. In 1925, following successful tests which were observed and vouched for by other scientists, he applied for a patent but his application was refused. The *Stromerzeuger* consisted of a number of magnets, flat coils and copper plates that were connected to a circuit which was initially powered by a small dry battery. The output from this was employed to light lamps and the power received was greater than the original electrical input.

In 1933, Coler made a larger version of the device which gave an output of 70 watts. By 1937, a still larger version had been built which produced 6 kilowatts. In 1943, Coler's device was tested by the research department of the OKM. Heinz Frohlich was ordered to work with Coler on testing and developing the *Stromerzeuger*. He investigated the energy changes that took place when the inductor circuits opened or closed, but failed to find any explanation that conformed to orthodox scientific theories. The device worked but neither Coler nor Frohlich could explain how or why.

In 1944 Coler was placed by the OKM with Continental Metall AG to undertake further research and development, but the worsening military situation meant that this never happened. Then in 1945 the *Stromerzeuger* was destroyed in an Allied bombing raid.

At the end of the war, Coler was interrogated by the British authorities, but he had no explanation as to why his devices worked. Coler suggested that perhaps ferromagnetism was an oscillating phenomenon, which took place in the magnetic circuit and that this created further oscillations in the electrical circuits of the devices. His only other idea was that perhaps he was drawing upon some unknown source of power, for which he suggested the name *Raumenergie* (space energy).

Whatever the true explanation, there is no doubt that his devices worked and both German and British scientists were able to test and observe their operation, but were equally baffled as to how and why they operated.

KARL SCHAPPELLER'S UR-MACHINE

Karl Schappeller was a dowser who met Himmler in 1933 and was recruited to work for the SS. One of the areas the Nazis were particularly interested in was attempting to make Germany self-sufficient in terms of its energy production. The RAG (Reich Works Association) claimed in 1930 that Schappeller's ideas might enable it to eliminate the national grid for electricity and that certainly appealed to the Nazis.

Schappeller's device was composed of two separate units. One was called the stator which was ball-shaped and consisted of two half-shells of steel. At each pole of the ball, a bar magnet was attached and at the centre of the sphere there was a space between the two magnets. Two internal coils made of hollow copper tube were wound within the central area. The copper tube was filled with a secret substance – presumably a fluid – known as the 'electret'. Electrical connections were then made, either to a battery or to an 'Ur-machine' (see below). The type of magnetism involved in this device was apparently not the normal ferromagnetism or electromagnetism but a much stronger type of magnetic energy.

It is not known what the mysterious substance known as electret was, but a Japanese professor has made a modern version using a mixture of resin, carnauba wax and beeswax. He stored it in a strong electrical field and heated it until it turned to a solid form.

The air was pumped out of the hollow core of Schappeller's sphere to create a vacuum. The ball was then mounted on a swivel device to enable the magnetic poles to be moved into different positions. The stator was able to function without the rotor and could apparently produce electrical energy on its own. By using the rotor further electrical energy could be produced so it was in essence a booster.

A 1930 publication, *Vril, the Cosmic Elementary Power*, by Johannes Täufer, refers to another form of the device, which Täufer calls an Ur-machine. This was said to consist of six spherical units with five revolving around the other sphere and a seventh unit used to rotate the five rotating spheres. The sixth and seventh spheres acted as an anode and a cathode to ground the unit. It could also activate other spheres without the necessity of using a battery.

Schappeller claimed that his device could power a ship or any other type of mechanical application. In his view, it was the 'glowing magnetism' that his machine could attain that set it apart from other devices. This was an immensely powerful magnetic field within the vacuum at the centre of the device and once it had been established the machine could be completely disconnected and would continue to function on its own. According to Schappeller's calculations, the energy produced by this 'glowing magnetism' was a thousand times more powerful than ordinary magnetism. He also claimed that the magnetism radiated outwards while the electrical current remained static.

During the last years of the Weimar Republic funding was made available to Schappeller for work on his device. Himmler's interest meant that under the Nazis he was given more extensive support and resources. He became a rich man because of this government investment.

The British engineer Cyril Davson examined the Schappeller device and spent three years working with Schappeller on his project. He believed that energy was drawn through the magnets into the glowing magnetic field in the vacuum at the centre and then radiated outwards. Davson, like Schappeller, subscribed to the notion of ether physics and believed that it was the nature of the ether that explained the otherwise mysterious working of the device.

XERUM 525 (RED MERCURY)

Red mercury is a curious substance that came into the public consciousness during the chaos that followed the end of the Cold War. There is considerable dispute over whether or not it exists and there are even more arguments about its origins and chemical constituents. It is said to be a conventional explosive, which has the power to create nuclear fusion without the need for an atomic bomb.

According to Russian scientists: 'It is a powder which is dark red in colour. But we irradiate it in a nuclear reactor which turns it into a very heavy liquid.' The same Russian sources claim that red mercury can be used to detonate a core of plutonium and consequently make 'the fissioning more efficient'.

Red mercury is said to be able to function 'with a tiny type of nuclear warhead'. This, however, is impossible when using conventional uranium and plutonium-based missiles.

There are various accounts of its chemical composition. A KGB report declared that it was 'a mercury salt of antinomy' and that it had been tested at the Dubna reactor, which was 'suited to implanting the material with strontium, caesium and other isotopes'.

Bulgarian scientists analysed a substance claimed to be red mercury and identified it as a mixture of mercury and tellurium. Scientists in South Africa came to a different conclusion, claiming that mercury antinomy oxide 'with a stick of uranium down the middle' was used.

British physicist Frank Barnaby discovered from Russian research that the mercury antinomy oxide was

> *dissolved in ordinary mercury metal, the type used in thermometers. It was then put in containers which were placed in the heart of a nuclear reactor for about 20 days. Under intense neutron bombardment, and perhaps with the addition of catalysts, the material was transformed and became a very thick and cherry-red liquid.*

According to an article in *Pravda* in 1993, red mercury is 'a super-conductive material used for producing high-precision conventional and nuclear bomb explosives, "stealth" surfaces and self-guided warheads'. A Channel 4 documentary claimed that: 'Russian scientists have designed a miniature neutron bomb using a mysterious compound called red mercury.'

Samuel T. Cohen, an American nuclear physicist, claimed that red mercury is produced through 'mixing special nuclear materials in very small amounts into the ordinary compound and then inserting the mixture into a nuclear reactor or bombarding it with a particle-accelerator beam'. Cohen declared that this process leads to temperatures 'that are capable of igniting the heavy hydrogen and producing a pure-fusion mini neutron bomb'.

The general consensus among those who believe in the reality of red mercury is that it began as a Nazi secret scientific programme and was a Soviet development of German work. Many German atomic scientists were captured by the Russians and ordered to work on their behalf. The mysterious substance known as Xerum 525, said to have been used in the Bell project (a secret Nazi device whose function is the subject of wildly varying speculation), is identified by many with the better known red mercury.

The precise composition of Xerum 525 is unknown. Most accounts believe that it was a mixture of mercury antinomy oxide that was then dissolved in mercury. Others suggest that its components include thorium and beryllium oxides. These materials were then subjected to bombardment by a particle-accelerator beam to produce a nuclear reaction.

The advantage of this process is that it enabled much smaller and lighter masses to be used to create a nuclear weapon. There remains considerable dispute over how effective it was, particularly during the war when heavy Allied bombing destroying many Nazi facilities and scientists were working under pressure of time.

Following Germany's surrender and the transfer of many of its leading nuclear scientists to Russian control, it is probable that further research and development of these promising and partially successful experiments was carried out in the Soviet Union. The result may well have been red mercury, or Xerum 525.

If that is true it would be another example of a Nazi project that was improved upon by other nations when wartime difficulties no longer applied.

NAZI SECRETS HANDED TO RUSSIANS

One of the most important Nazi factories was the military research facility at the Skoda works in Czechoslovakia. From 1938 to early 1945 it was run by Dr Wilhelm Voss and its scientists and engineers worked at the cutting edge of science. One of its most advanced projects was the development of nuclear-powered aircraft. Lasers and rockets were also key fields of research and had reached a high degree of sophistication by the time the war ended.

The 6th May 1945 saw this prized state-of-the-art research centre in the hands of the US Army and British and American intelligence teams moved on to the site to explore its riches. For eight years the Skoda works had developed numerous advanced projects and the Western Allies were eager to take full advantage of their discovery.

That at least was the intention. Unfortunately, the leading players in the exiled Czechoslovak government had already been forced into an alliance with the Soviet Union in 1943. The government in exile had agreed that the Czechs would be in the Russian sphere of influence after the war. In January 1945, the OSS produced an intelligence report stating that Czech Communists and Social Democrats were 'willing and anxious to see Czechoslovakia more or less completely integrated with and dependent on Soviet policy'. It concluded with astonishing naïvety that: 'Czech émigrés are convinced that the USSR will not impose either the economic or political methods of Russian Communism on Czechoslovakia.'

At this point, it is worth making a brief detour into the history of Europe after the end of World War I. Various new countries had emerged out of the defeat of Germany, Austria and the Ottoman Empire. In terms of Europe, Poland, Czechoslovakia, Albania, Yugoslavia, Romania, Bulgaria and Hungary had been carved out of parts of Russia and most of Austria and Germany. Danzig, overwhelmingly German, had been made an 'international city' and Memel, also overwhelmingly German, had been ceded to the newly independent nation of Lithuania, becoming Klaipėda.

Of all these new nations, only Czechoslovakia had succeeded in establishing a genuinely free and democratic country. Poland, Albania and Hungary were military dictatorships, while Romania, Bulgaria and Yugoslavia were quasi-democratic but prone to frequent bouts of authoritarian rule. The Czechs, however, under the benevolent presidency of Thomas Masaryk, had managed to establish a genuine and successful democracy. His successors tried to maintain its independence in the face of aggression by Hitler but failed. By 1939 the whole country had become part of the German Reich.

Under the terms of the Atlantic Charter in 1941, all of the countries of eastern Europe that had been annexed by the Nazis were supposed to be restored to democratic control at the end of the war. Stalin was prepared to pay lip service to that ideal – particularly in 1941 when the war in Russia was not going well for the Soviet Union – but had no intention of implementing those policies once eastern Europe was firmly under his control. By 1948, he had succeeded in taking over every country in the region except Yugoslavia and Albania which, though they became Communist states, retained their independence from Moscow.

The extent to which Soviet agents had penetrated eastern Europe during the war made it much harder for the Western Allies to work successfully in those countries.

Allies obstructed

As a result, when the Americans and the British reached Skoda with the intention of discovering and using its secrets they found themselves obstructed at every turn. The Czech workers had been well treated by Voss and were not anxious to assist the Allies. Soviet agents also advised the workers not to co-operate with them, reminding them that the plant would soon be in Russian hands and that their actions during this 'transitional stage' would be closely monitored by their new masters.

The British learned that copies of all documents and drawings had been microfilmed and transferred to a nearby location and demanded access to them, but the Czechs at the plant flatly denied that any such microfilms ever existed.

Every attempt to elicit information produced the same excuse, that 'all equipment and records' had been destroyed. The British failed to extract any information from the Czech workers at Skoda, but the Americans were marginally more successful and managed to secure two missiles and some scientific data.

Further examples of deliberate disruption by Skoda employees were the sudden 'unavailability' of transport vehicles to take Western inspection teams to visit various subsidiary plants. By September 1945, all of them were fully controlled by the Soviet Union and all information had been channelled directly to Moscow. These included factories producing machine tools, diesel engines and electrical equipment, car factories, shipyards and a gun factory. Even before Skoda had passed officially into Russian hands, it was already building hydrofoils and submarine propellers for the Soviet Navy. The recalcitrance of the Czech employees may have been unexpected, but it certainly robbed the West of some of the most advanced German secret projects.

That much is certain and was beyond the control of the Western Allies. What happened on 10 May, however, was entirely different. Either through incompetence, a blind obedience to orders or as part of a conscious strategy, its consequences affected Europe for the next 40 years.

Was a US officer working for the Russians?

On 10 May, Voss travelled to Skoda. The workers there still held him in high esteem and he set out on a dangerous mission to the plant. As he said in 1949:

> I had hoped that I would be able to convince the American officers in charge of the plant, pending its handing over to the Red Army, that a saving of whatever could be saved of the very advanced research data and blueprints was a matter of prime importance to American national defence. Once the material had fallen into Soviet hands, all this technology would obviously become a threat to Western security.

Voss went to the plant and was recognized by some former employees, who allowed him to enter. He made contact with staff and discovered that the most important documents were sitting in a truck. He then approached the American officer in charge and told him it was crucial to evacuate the material before the Soviets arrived to take possession. The officer refused and told Voss that he had been instructed to allow the Red Army to take over everything. Voss responded that he had risked his life to go there and that it was not in the interests of the United States to allow these key documents to fall into the hands of the Russians.

He pointed out that at the Mittelwerk facility at Nordhausen the Americans had taken charge of aeronautical and rocket parts and data and those were being shipped to America. This operation had clearly been authorized by the US government and the material in the Skoda factory was equally valuable.

In fact, though Voss could not have known this, a directive by the US Joint Chiefs of Staff on 24 April 1945 had instructed military personnel to 'preserve from destruction and take under your control all records, plans, notes, documents, scientific information and data, belonging to German organizations engaged in military research'. Voss's point, therefore, though made in ignorance of this directive, was entirely valid.

The US officer remained unmoved. He retorted that an American team had been to the plant that week and removed two rocket missiles, so they had presumably taken 'all they needed'. Voss persisted and suggested that the officer should contact US intelligence, but again he was met with a flat refusal.

Undeterred, he spent the night at the Skoda plant and two days later saw its handover to the Red Army. Voss and two former colleagues then tried to drive the truck with the top secret data out of the facility, but they were spotted. Both US and Russian officers ordered them to stop. The last chance to save German secret projects for the West had been lost. This material included nuclear weapons data and advanced aircraft and missile projects.

The question remains – was this obstructionism by the American officer simply a failure to grasp the importance of the material at Skoda or was he acting under orders from Washington? If he had not been given an order, was it simply a case of personal obstinacy or an unwillingness to involve US intelligence in the proceedings? Or could it perhaps have been something more sinister – was the officer a Communist sympathizer?

The true answers to these questions may never be known. Czech obstructionism is understandable, but the American attitude is much harder to comprehend. Whatever led to the officer's fateful decision to refuse the request to transport the Skoda documents to the West, the repercussions were dramatic and lasting.

CHAPTER SEVEN
THE RIDDLE OF RUDOLF HESS

Rudolf Hess for a time was one of the most powerful and influential men in Germany. He fought in World War I initially as a soldier, but then switched to the air force and became a skilled pilot. After Germany's defeat in the war, he joined a number of groups that opposed the Weimar Republic and, by 1920, he had gravitated towards the Nazi Party after hearing Hitler speak. Hess became convinced that Hitler was the saviour of Germany. An early member of the Party, he took part in the abortive Munich putsch in 1923 and was imprisoned in Landsberg Prison along with Hitler. During their imprisonment, Hess, who drew much of his inspiration from the *völkisch* thinker Karl Haushofer, collaborated with Hitler and his mentor in the writing of *Mein Kampf*.

Hess was fiercely loyal to Hitler and said in 1934: 'One man remains beyond criticism and that is the Führer.' He was a shy and reserved man who found public speaking difficult, but Wilhelm Bohle, who headed an organization to represent Germans living abroad, stated that Hess was 'the biggest idealist we have had in Germany'.

Unlike the cynical Goering, Goebbels, Bormann and Heydrich or the often contradictory Himmler, Hess was a 'true believer'. The problem was that he was too gullible, not only swallowing Nazi racial mythology but also a cocktail of esoteric ideas. Although he was still officially one of the most powerful men in Germany, before long he was increasingly sidelined and not taken seriously. He certainly had far less grasp on reality than most Nazi leaders.

In spite of these defects, Hitler made Hess his deputy and he was a close personal friend for many years. His attitude began to change in 1938, however, when the *Kristallnacht* pogroms – which led to brutal violence against the Jews in Germany – shocked him deeply. With the growing influence of men like Goebbels, Bormann and Himmler, the idealistic Hess began to lose even more influence and became increasingly irrelevant. He was wheeled out for ceremonial events, but had little practical input into affairs in Germany.

In 1936, Hess met the Duke of Hamilton at the Berlin Olympics. Hess spoke fluent English and believed he had struck up a friendship with the aristocrat. Hamilton, like many British nobles of the time, certainly had pro-German sympathies, but Hess's belief that Hamilton could be a useful intermediary with the British government was, of course, mistaken. Hamilton's former membership of the Anglo-German Friendship Society counted for nothing in the duke's eyes once the two countries were at war.

Hamilton's appointment in 1940 as Lord Steward of the Royal Household aroused Hess's interest. As a German whose own experience of monarchy was the autocratic rule of the Kaiser, he could not grasp that George VI was a purely constitutional monarch and had no power to direct government policy. So even

Rudolf Hess sits next to Hitler at the Congress of National Labour, Berlin, c.1935.

if Hamilton had proposed a compromise peace to the king, the monarch had no power to act on that advice.

FLIGHT TO BRITAIN

In 1940 Hess began to plan his mission to Britain. He began by asking Haushofer's son Albrecht to write to the Duke of Hamilton and propose a meeting between them in Portugal or Switzerland. The duke never received the letter, but MI5 intercepted it and immediately began investigating Hamilton for possible disloyalty.

Meanwhile, Hess was already planning for a worst-case scenario in which he had to meet the duke in Scotland. He learned to fly a Messerschmitt Me 110 fighter-bomber and asked for it to be adapted for long-range flying.

On 10 May 1941, Hess reached the Messerschmitt airfield in Augsburg, where he announced his intention of flying to Norway. Before boarding the plane, he handed four letters to a companion. One was addressed to Hitler, another to Hess's wife, the third to Messerschmitt and the fourth to a fellow pilot. He left the airfield at 5.45 p.m.

From that point onwards, there is considerable controversy about his actions. Even with the modifications made to his aircraft by Messerschmitt, it has been claimed that it could not have flown from Augsburg to Scotland without refuelling. Hess certainly claimed that he had flown non-stop, but that is difficult to believe. Even if external fuel tanks had been fitted to the plane, it still lacked sufficient fuel for him to have reached his destination. An examination of the aircraft wreckage showed that it had not been fitted with external fuel tanks, so Hess would have been unable to fly further than about half the distance.

The logical conclusion is that Hess must have stopped some-where to refuel. Aalborg in Denmark is the most likely destination, but Norway is also a possibility. In either case, he would have needed assistance and it has been suggested that Albrecht Haushofer, who was strongly anti-Nazi and was involved in the German Resistance to Hitler, might have had a hand in Hess's mission. It is also possible that the equally anti-Nazi Admiral Canaris may have been involved.

Whatever the true facts, Hess's Messerschmitt ran out of fuel near the Scottish village of Eaglesham. The plane crashed at 11.09 p.m. and its pilot bailed out and was arrested shortly after he had parachuted to safety. He gave his name as Captain Albert Horn and was taken to Maryhill barracks in Glasgow for questioning. While being interrogated, he asked to speak to the Duke of Hamilton.

The baffled duke insisted that he knew no one called Albert Horn, but he still went to the barracks to meet the prisoner. Hess immediately declared that he had met Hamilton at the Berlin Olympics and they had lunched together. The prisoner then said: 'I do not know if you recognize me, but I am Rudolf Hess.'

The two men talked for a while and Hess tried to persuade Hamilton to put forward his proposals for peace between their countries. But Hess's entreaties fell on deaf ears and the duke told him that the government could not possibly agree to his terms. He left Hess in custody and returned home.

THEORIES SURROUNDING HESS'S FLIGHT

As well as the unresolved question of how Hess made the flight to Scotland at all, further mysteries surround his journey. Was it truly an unauthorized mission or had it been undertaken with the full knowledge and support of Hitler? Had Hess become so disillusioned with Hitler and the Nazis that he had defected to Britain? Was the pilot who bailed out over Scotland the 'real' Hess or an imposter? Finally, was the whole affair leading up to his doomed flight the result of a British intelligence 'sting' to lure him to Britain?

All of these questions have been hotly disputed and there is some evidence in favour of three of them. The idea that the airman who landed in Scotland was an imposter can, however, be ruled out. Even so, there are three main variants of the theory, none of them feasible.

One version has the 'real' Hess being murdered by the British and replaced with a double. The Nuremberg Trials alone refute that. Goering and Speer knew Hess well and would have seized on the opportunity to expose an imposter.

Another version has Himmler killing the 'real' Hess and replacing him with a double. But there is no reason why Himmler would have done such a thing and it would not have been easy to find a pilot who was a lookalike. The Nuremberg Trials once again refute that idea. The man in the dock certainly was Rudolf Hess.

The third variation on this implausible theme is that Hess never left Germany and a pilot doubled for him. It is claimed that Hess remained out of sight and a cover story was issued. Apart from the inherent unlikelihood of such a pointless course of action, the Nuremberg Trials show that the 'real' Hess was tried and convicted.

A slightly modified version of the 'double' theory suggests that after his trial and conviction at Nuremberg Hess was exchanged for a lookalike. A motive for this is difficult to determine. And why would someone take Hess's place at Spandau Prison and keep up the pretence for the rest of his life? Hess in Spandau behaved exactly like the 'real' Hess.

The idea that Hitler knew of and approved Hess's flight is also contrary to the evidence. Hitler was baffled and angry and assumed – possibly correctly – that Hess had gone mad. If

Hess had received help from anyone in his failed mission it was certainly not Hitler.

The other two theories – that Hess defected to Britain or that he was lured there by British intelligence – are more plausible. Hess had been shocked by the violence of the 1938 pogrom against the Jews and he was an idealist who despised his fellow Nazis for using their power to enrich themselves. In addition, he might at least have sensed or heard talk of the planned invasion of Russia and believed that it would lead to the end of National Socialism. All of these factors may have played a part and his own growing marginalization among the German leadership may also have led him to defect.

However, there is no hard evidence that his flight to Britain was a conscious defection and if it had been then his imprisonment by the British would have been for a war crime. Hess and Speer often talked during their years as fellow inmates in Spandau and Speer discussed the flight to Britain with Hess. Speer was not released until 1966 and in all of that time Hess never told Speer that he had flown to Britain with the intention of defecting, so on balance that idea must be rejected.

There remain only two other possible explanations. One is the 'official' version in which Hess acted alone out of a quixotic belief that he could use his imagined personal influence with British contacts who had been Nazi sympathizers before the war. The other is the idea that he was lured into a trap in an elaborate operation masterminded by British intelligence.

WAS HESS LURED BY BRITISH INTELLIGENCE?

Before examining the specific question of whether Hess's flight might have come about as the result of a British intelligence 'sting', it is necessary to consider various unofficial peace feelers put out by elements in both British and German circles through the medium of Carl Burckhardt, the Swiss president of the Red Cross. Burckhardt had asked the British government whether they would be willing to make peace with Germany, and if so on what terms. The British response was that the Germans had to restore the independence of the occupied countries. It was also an essential precondition of peace talks that Hitler must stand down as German leader.

On 28 April 1941, Albrecht Haushofer travelled to Switzerland to meet Burckhardt. In the meantime, independently or perhaps with Haushofer's knowledge, Himmler contacted Burckhardt and asked if the British would be willing to make peace with a government led by him rather than Hitler.

Meanwhile the military situation, for the first time since the beginning of the war, began to turn against the Axis powers. Mussolini overreached himself in North Africa and Greece, British troops began to push the Italians back in Africa and the Greeks forced the invading army out of their country in ignominious retreat.

The Italian reversals infuriated Hitler, but made Himmler – who had at least one spy inside Haushofer's German Resistance group – more willing to approach the British indirectly. This was the first of many occasions when Himmler contemplated a coup to overthrow Hitler. On the other hand, Mussolini's failures strengthened British resolve and made Churchill less willing to compromise.

In spite of the popular support Churchill enjoyed in 1941, his own party contained people who not only disliked and distrusted him but also saw Stalin as a greater threat than Hitler. The war had reached stalemate, with the Germans unable to advance and the British unable to launch a successful attack on Germany. In these circumstances, the idea of making peace with a Germany without Hitler appealed to many of those people.

It was to this mindset that Haushofer and Hess hoped to appeal. Haushofer was at least genuinely anti-Nazi and also regarded Burckhardt of the Red Cross as a trustworthy and neutral intermediary.

Burckhardt was genuinely appalled at the prospect of widening the war to include Russia and possibly the United States and Japan. Meanwhile, British intelligence officers interviewed the Duke of Hamilton. They were aware that before the war he had been friendly with Haushofer and had also met Hess, so MI6 suggested that Hamilton should meet Haushofer in Portugal.

In April 1941, Hess, who was totally opposed to a two-front war, met Haushofer several times and on 28 April Haushofer met Burckhardt.

There is clear evidence that British intelligence, whether through Haushofer or Burckhardt, knew that any messages passed on to Germany via them would reach Hess and probably even Himmler. But whether MI6 was planning a conscious 'sting' to lure Hess to Britain is uncertain.

In favour of that theory is the curious case of *The Flying Visit*. This humorous novel, written by Peter Fleming, brother of Ian, was published in 1940. During the war both men were involved in intelligence work, including such successful examples of deception as Operation Mincemeat.

Fleming's novel imagined Hitler flying to Britain, landing and at first being mistaken for a comedian parodying the Nazi leader. His true identity is eventually recognized and he is arrested. Unsure what to do with him, in the end the British return him to Germany.

There are significant differences between the novel and Hess's flight. Fleming imagined Hitler landing rather than his deputy. Also, Hitler makes no attempt to contact Nazi sympathizers in *The*

Flying Visit, while Hess certainly tried to meet a man he believed would be willing to co-operate with him. Nor, of course, was Hess returned to Germany as Hitler was in Fleming's novel. It is also difficult to believe that Fleming or MI6 would have 'telegraphed' a plot to lure Hess to Britain by writing and publishing the book.

There is no doubt that Burckhardt and Haushofer were used by British intelligence, possibly as channels of disinformation. They were also anxious to learn any possible information that their intermediaries might pass on. But the idea that Hess was deliberately enticed to Britain by MI6 is more difficult to accept. What would be the motive for such a plot? How would Britain benefit from taking him prisoner?

Even as a propaganda coup, the British government failed to exploit Hess's capture. A brief period when it made the headlines was followed by a total lack of media interest. Churchill's response on hearing of the arrest was: 'Hess or no Hess, I'm going to watch the Marx Brothers.' This shows how little importance he attached to the event. When all of the evidence is considered, while MI6 may have tried to use Hess in other ways, it is highly improbable that there was ever a conscious British plot to lure him to the United Kingdom.

For all its difficulties and implausibility, the 'official' version of Hess's flight remains the most probable explanation. Hess, acting on his own initiative, believed that he could succeed in making a peace treaty with Britain. He certainly did not expect to be arrested on his arrival but imagined that he would be treated as an envoy of the German government and be accorded the protocols of diplomatic immunity. Instead, he was treated as a prisoner of war and spent the rest of his life incarcerated.

Even though MI6 may have deliberately misled Hess via Burckhardt and Haushofer into overestimating the strength of

British opposition to the war, Hess alone took the decision to fly to Britain in a desperate search for peace. So it seems that all of the various conspiracy theories in the field ultimately fail.

MYSTERIOUS DEATH

The final mystery in the case of Hess concerns his death. On 17 August 1987, at the age of 93, Hess allegedly hanged himself at Spandau Prison. By this stage of his life, he was barely able to stand or walk and could hardly tie his shoelaces. The idea that this frail man could have hanged himself is difficult, if not almost impossible, to believe.

Hess is alleged to have hanged himself with an electrical extension cable in the summerhouse located in the grounds of the prison. The official documents surrounding his death – most of which remain classified – state:

> *The extension cable used had for some time been kept in the summerhouse, and when not in use (so that a standard lamp could be put in the position Hess likes) it was tied to the window with a knot. There was thus no need for Hess to remove it from anywhere.*

Prisons routinely seek to prevent inmates from accessing anything which they could use to harm or kill themselves. Hess had been in prison for over 40 years and had made other attempts at suicide. A flexible lead extension is quite suitable for that purpose and yet it was left in the cabin when Hess was unattended. This is unquestionably criminal negligence at best. Nor is the photograph of the lead credible. It is a boating tool designed to hold heavy weights and is hardly the type of lead one would expect to find in prison.

Shortly before Hess's death his flying suit and other personal items were stolen from the prison, demonstrating that security at Spandau was astonishingly lax. In 1986, there was even an explosion which destroyed an annex of the prison.

Only a partial transcript of the minutes of the governors' meeting at Spandau has been released. The investigation they carried out into Hess's death remains classified and the autopsy report was not released until 2017. It mentions briefly – without explanation – a mysterious bruise found on Hess's head.

No attempt was even made to investigate any possible link between the theft of Hess's possessions and his death soon afterwards. Not even fingerprints were taken from the cabin where he died. Even the summerhouse itself was, according to the British governor of the prison, 'crushed and destroyed'. It was also claimed that the cord had been destroyed along with the summerhouse. All of these highly suspicious moves occurred within 48 hours of Hess's death.

The overwhelming probability is that Hess was murdered but the question remains – why? What threat did this 93-year-old man pose that led to his murder? Who stood to gain from his death?

In spite of the clear evidence of a cover-up by the British and American authorities at Spandau, it is difficult to imagine why they would want to murder Hess. The truth could be that one of the guards, perhaps following his earlier theft of personal items, demanded more 'souvenirs' from Hess. Maybe Hess refused and was killed and the guard then faked his death to resemble suicide. The authorities might then have gone along with the deception from a reluctance to expose incompetence and corruption.

The true story of Rudolf Hess – both in life and death – may never be known. It is, however, one of the most bizarre and fascinating mysteries from that era.

CHAPTER EIGHT

MYSTERIES OF THE SEA

MYSTERY SUBMARINES

When the German government surrendered to the Allies, it ordered all of its combatant forces to lay down their arms and hand themselves over. However, three U-boat crews refused to obey these commands. The captain of *U-1277* scuttled his boat off the coast of Portugal on 3 June 1945 and the Portuguese government interned the crew; the crew of *U-530* sailed across the Atlantic Ocean before surrendering to the Argentine authorities at Mar del Plata on 10 July 1945; and *U-977* reached the same port on 17 August before she was also surrendered to the Argentines.

Why did the crews of these two U-boats refuse to capitulate to the Allies? What made them choose the same port in the same country? Why were the two surrenders a month apart?

For years, there has been speculation about the actions and motives of the submarine crews. The theory that they took Hitler, Bormann and other Nazi leaders to a safe place of exile has always been popular. Others believe that the U-boats carried Nazi treasure, Nazi relics or secret documents.

Where was *U-530*?

First Lieutenant Otto Wermuth was in command of *U-530*. He decided not to surrender to the Allies but instead headed for the neutral country of Argentina. On 10 July 1945 he surrendered his vessel to the Argentine Navy.

There are many curious aspects of the submarine crew's conduct which remain unexplained. First of all, Wermuth jettisoned the deck gun. Then the vessel's log was missing and the crew carried no form of identification. Even more baffling was the duration of the U-boat's journey. It took a month longer than it should for them to reach Argentina.

This delay has led to an assortment of theories. The most popular and persistent of them is the idea that the submarine was used to ferry Hitler and other leading Nazis to a secret location. A variety of personnel and destinations have been suggested.

Two Brazilian admirals put forward different theories. Admiral Jorge Dodsworth Martins claimed that *U-530* had sunk the cruiser *Bahia* while Admiral Dudal Teixeira believed that the submarine had gone to Argentina after first sailing to Japan.

The suggestion that *U-530* sank the *Bahia* was quickly disproved. An inquiry into its sinking found that the cause was a gunnery accident.

Crew members of the submarine U-530 *at a detention centre near Miami in 1945; on the far right is the commander, Lieutenant Otto Wermuth.*

The Argentine naval ministry went even further. They issued an official statement which not only exonerated the submarine from the sinking of the *Bahia* but added that no Nazi leaders or senior military personnel were present on the vessel. The communiqué went on to say that no one had been landed on the coast of Argentina before *U-530* surrendered.

Conspiracy theories about the escape of Hitler to South America via a U-boat surfaced as early as July 1945. The Hungarian journalist Ladislao Szabó had emigrated to Argentina and that month saw him post an article in the newspaper *Critica*.

Szabó claimed that Hitler had escaped from Germany in a U-boat. After landing in Argentina he had made his way to Patagonia and eventually to a secret Nazi 'fortress' in the Neu Schwabenland region of Antarctica. This theory gathered momentum after the arrival of *U-530* in Argentina.

Szabó produced a book in 1947, *Hitler esta vivo* (Hitler is Alive), in which he originated both the U-boat escape theories and the idea of a Nazi stronghold in Antarctica. In 2006 he produced a second book, *Hitler no murió en el búnker* (Hitler Did Not Die in the Bunker).

What is true is that *U-530* remained at sea for a month longer than necessary to complete its journey. There is no obvious reason either for the time spent voyaging or for the destruction of identity papers, the vessel's log and the submarine's deck gun. It is just possible to imagine that the commander jettisoned the gun in case he was approached by enemy vessels, but there is no logical explanation for concealing the identity of the crew or for destroying the log.

Whether or not this submarine carried treasures or Nazi leaders to safety will never be known. The actions of the commander of the U-boat remain inexplicable. Unless he had something to hide there is no obvious reason for destroying the log book or the identity papers of the crew. Whatever his secret may have been Wermuth took it with him to his grave.

U-977's 'underwater record'

An equally baffling case is the final voyage of U-977. This submarine was built in Hamburg in 1943 and used as a training vessel for crews in the Baltic Sea until February 1945. It was then moved to Kristiansand in Norway and, on 2 May, set out on its first combat mission in the English Channel.

Two days later, it received an order to avoid engaging the enemy and, on 9 May, it was formally commanded to surrender to the Allies. First Lieutenant Heinz Schäffer was in charge of the vessel and he discussed his orders with the crew. Most of the 48 crew members refused to surrender and agreed to sail to Argentina. However, 16 crew members preferred to take their chances and were disembarked off the coast of Norway, at the island of Holsnøy near Bergen, on 10 May 1945. They landed on life rafts and surrendered to the Norwegian authorities.

The remaining crew members sailed across the Atlantic Ocean until they arrived at Mar del Plata on the coast of Argentina. There they surrendered to the Argentine authorities on 17 August 1945.

Schäffer and his crew were initially interned in Argentina before being handed over to the Americans. The same process had been carried out with the crew of U-530. They became prisoners of war before being transferred to Britain and then finally released and returned to Germany in 1946.

Schäffer was repeatedly interrogated about the circumstances of his voyage and in particular why his journey from Norway to Argentina had taken so long. It had taken 108 days for them to make the voyage from Norway to Argentina. He claimed that the vessel had spent 66 days submerged throughout its voyage across the

Atlantic Ocean. They had then stopped at the Cape Verde Islands on 14 July for a short break before continuing their journey, passing the equator on 23 July 1945. There are inconsistencies both in Schäffer's story and the various accounts of it given by the authorities who interviewed him. Some versions claim that the U-boat spent only 99 days at sea, while others record a time of 108 days.

The US Navy report on the incident makes no mention of a 66-day voyage underwater. It is short on detail and its reliability as a source has been questioned, particularly in terms of the possible mistranslation of some of the German crew's testimony.

The crew's accounts seem to support the idea that they spent 66 days submerged. They also agree that the submarine made a brief stop in the Cape Verde Islands before being forced to continue its journey with only one functioning engine.

As with *U-530*, *U-977*'s delayed arrival in Argentina gave huge publicity to the conspiracy theories of Szabó and his imitators. The idea that one or both of the submarines – or even a whole fleet of U-boats – had carried Hitler, Eva Braun, Bormann and other Nazi leaders became extremely popular. So did the suggestion that the vessels had ferried looted treasure or secret documents.

Unlike Wermuth, Schäffer had not jettisoned his deck guns or destroyed the vessel's log and the crew's identity papers. What evidence is available – though sparse and at times contradictory – suggests that he was telling the truth about his submarine's remarkable journey with the U-boat submerged for most of its voyage.

With Schäffer it appears that the 'mystery' voyage of his submarine was really a remarkable feat of seamanship rather than concealing some hidden purpose. Wermuth's behaviour is harder to explain and the deliberate destruction of crucial evidence strongly suggests that he had something to hide.

On 25 September 1946, the Agence France-Presse said: 'The continuous rumours about German U-boat activity in the region of Tierra del Fuego between the southernmost tip of Latin America and the continent of Antarctica are based on true happenings.'

The French newspaper *France-Soir* described a curious encounter with a German U-boat nearly two years after the war had finished. It reported:

> *Almost one and a half years after cessation of hostilities in Europe, the Icelandic Whaler* Juliana *was stopped by a large German U-boat. The* Juliana *was in the Antarctic region around Malvinas Islands [the Falklands] when a German submarine surfaced and raised the German official Flag of Mourning – red with a black edge.*
>
> *The submarine commander sent out a boarding party, which approached the* Juliana *in a rubber dinghy, and having boarded the whaler demanded of Capt. Hekla part of his fresh food stocks. The request was made in the definite tone of an order to which resistance would have been unwise.*

The German officer spoke in English and paid for his supplies in dollars. He also told the whaler of the location of a school of whales and the captain of the whaler later discovered them in the designated location.

This story has become an urban legend on the internet but it is untrue. Icelandic whalers have never operated in the Antarctic region and there was never an Icelandic whaling ship called the *Juliana*. The name of the alleged captain of the vessel is also suspicious as Hekla is the name of a volcano on Iceland. Either this story is an exercise in creative journalism or the newspaper was misled by a hoaxer.

THE DESTRUCTION OF THE *NORMANDIE*

Another nautical mystery surrounds the destruction of the French liner *Normandie*. This luxury liner was one of the most prestigious passenger ships of its era. The advent of war in 1939 found the vessel near New York City and the captain decided to put into harbour and seek sanctuary in the United States.

The fall of France pushed the vessel's status into limbo. Pétain's Vichy government might have wished for its return, but the crew preferred to remain in their American exile. The ship's owners were paying berthing charges of $1,000 a day, while she remained idle in the harbour.

Most of the sailors were paid off by the company and only a skeleton crew remained. On 15 May 1941 the US Treasury Department ordered 150 coastguards to join the ship's company to 'ensure *Normandie*'s safety and guard against sabotage'. *Normandie* remained in this in-between state until December 1941, the month when the US entered the war. The day after war between Germany and the US was declared saw an abrupt change in the status of the *Normandie*, when the coastguards took full possession of the vessel and the decision was taken to convert her into a troopship.

This prospect had been anticipated with apprehension by the Nazis for the previous two years. Admiral Wilhelm Canaris estimated that the ship could carry around 10,000 US soldiers to Europe in a single crossing of the Atlantic.

New York was full of Nazi spies and sympathizers, many of them working along the waterfront. One of the leading Nazi spies was Waldemar Othmer, who left Germany in 1919 and became a naturalized American. He worked in the Brooklyn Navy Yard, which gave him ample opportunity to pass on military secrets to Germany. Only in 1944 was he finally exposed as a German spy.

With the outbreak of war Nazi agents and sympathizers began to feed information back to Germany and minor acts of sabotage were also committed. The size of the *Normandie* made it impossible for the ship to be moved, so her conversion to a troopship took place in her mooring on Pier 88.

Hundreds of civilian workers were drafted in and the navy demanded that the *Normandie*'s remodelling should be completed by 14 February. The plan was to finish the work and sail the ship to Boston. From there the vessel, renamed by the US Navy the *Lafayette*, would sail to Northern Ireland and unload its first detachment of troops.

That was the plan but the work took far longer than anticipated. The designated captain of the *Lafayette* complained that he was expected to command the huge ship with around half the number 'required for the efficient operation of the vessel at sea'.

Pleas were made to the Navy Department to extend the conversion deadline for the ship. At first the navy seemed sympathetic but they then insisted that the work could not be delayed. A frantic race against time ensued, with workmen desperately trying to finish the vessel on schedule. The result was that 'corners had to be cut'.

The ship's potential captain protested about the quality of workmanship and the strain placed on the workmen. These protests led to the arrangement of a meeting with senior Navy Department officials to discuss the vessel's state of readiness – a meeting that never took place.

Accident or sabotage?

Events soon made all of the arguments irrelevant. At 2.30 p.m. on 8 February, the ship caught fire. Two men were working with an oxyacetylene torch and sparks from it hit a pile of life jackets.

The workmen tried to extinguish the flames, but there was no fire watch on board to help them. Because of the conversion, the fire alarms had been disconnected and the fire hose ran out of water almost immediately.

The blaze soon turned into a 'surging fire' that was impossible to control. Before long, the three upper decks of the ship were engulfed in flames. It took nearly half an hour before firefighters were able to access the vessel. They pumped 6,000 gallons (27,000 l) of water into the ship to try and quench the flames and eventually the fire was described as being 'under control'.

Unfortunately, so much water had been pumped into the vessel that it began to tilt. Desperate attempts to stabilize the ship failed and it finally capsized 12 hours after the fire began. President Roosevelt and many navy officials suspected sabotage by Nazi agents, but some years later another possibility emerged.

The Mafia boss Charles 'Lucky' Luciano claimed in his autobiography that he had given the order for the *Normandie* to be torched. He said he had devised the plan with other Mafia bosses to force the navy to allow his criminal organization to protect the docks.

Is this claim simply boastfulness after the event? There is no doubt that naval and US intelligence representatives met Mafia bosses after the demise of the *Normandie*. Luciano and his fellow bosses were certainly ruthless enough to have been willing to destroy a ship to further their agenda.

There was an official investigation by Congress that blamed the incident on 'carelessness', an 'absence of proper co-ordination' and 'undue haste'. Incompetence and negligence were blamed for the disaster rather than sabotage – by the Nazis or the Mafia.

There were certainly many opportunities for spying and sabotage at this early stage of the war. Luciano's men did effectively control the docks and they could easily have started a fire on the *Normandie*. Equally, the chaotic attempts to rush through the work needed to make the *Normandie* battle-ready led to carelessness. The last theory is borne out by the testimony of the two men whose acetylene torches started the fire.

The sinking of the *Normandie* may have been a tragic accident or the result of deliberate sabotage by the Nazis or the Mafia. We may never know the truth about its destruction.

WHO SANK THE *TANG*?

The USS *Tang* was one of the stars of the Pacific War. On its four previous missions, the submarine had sunk 31 Japanese vessels. Its fifth and final mission was on 24 October 1944.

The target was a Japanese convoy in the straits of Taiwan. In charge of the submarine, Commander Richard O'Kane was confident of further success. He stalked the convoy through the night and when morning came he surfaced in readiness to attack.

The United States Navy submarine, USS Tang.

The submarine was detected by the Japanese convoy and they attacked it. O'Kane manoeuvred his vessel until it was within 1,000 yards (914 m) of the enemy ships and then fired six torpedoes, all of which hit the target. Three Japanese destroyers advanced on the submarine, but O'Kane fired three more torpedoes as they approached. All three hit the ships and the *Tang* was able to escape in the chaos.

Only two torpedoes remained. O'Kane decided to use them to destroy the transport ships he had crippled earlier. Both torpedoes were released. The first hit its target, but the second torpedo behaved erratically. It started to head straight towards the *Tang*, instead of making for its intended target.

At first O'Kane assumed a Japanese submarine must have fired at him. He ordered the crew to take evasive action by manoeuvring out of the path of the torpedo. To his astonishment, however, the torpedo was not following a straight line. Instead, it was moving around the *Tang* in a series of ever-decreasing circles. The submarine had no way of escaping and was about to be sunk.

Desperate attempts were made to move the submarine outside that deadly circular path, but all efforts were in vain. As O'Kane recorded in his memoirs 30 years later:

> *The torpedo hit abreast the after torpedo room, close to the manoeuvring room bulkhead. The detonation was devastating, our stern going under before the topside watch could recover. Our ship sank by the stern in seconds. The seas rolled in from aft, washing us from the bridge and shears.*

The crew in the stern compartments died almost instantly. Many survivors imagined they had struck a mine. Nine crew members, including O'Kane, were thrown into the sea by the fury of the impact. No one had been able to put on a life jacket and only four of the nine swept overboard survived.

Thirty men remained trapped inside the submarine with its conning-tower hatch closed. The Japanese began dropping depth charges, but none were close enough to damage the doomed submarine.

A laborious and dangerous escape then took place. An inflatable dinghy was passed through the escape chamber and one by one the men followed it through. Not all of them were able to make it out and most of those who succeeded perished in the water. Out of a crew of 87 men only 15 survived.

Their ordeal was not yet over. The crew were picked up by a Japanese destroyer, but as soon as the Japanese crew realized they were American submariners they beat them angrily. They were then taken to Taiwan and held in a prison camp. Two days later, they were placed on another ship and sent to Japan. They remained in their new prison camp until 29 August 1945 and by that time only nine of the 15 survivors remained alive.

The US Navy had been baffled by the cause of the sinking as the Japanese did not appear to be responsible. O'Kane believed that it was a malfunctioning torpedo from the *Tang* that sank the submarine. That remains the most probable explanation for the mystery.

THE *CAP ARCONA* TRAGEDY

In May 1945 the war in Europe was almost over. Hitler was dead and his successor Admiral Karl Dönitz was preparing to surrender. But fighting still took place and the relentless Allied bombing campaign continued.

During this final phase of the war in Europe, a great human tragedy occurred. What seemed to be a normal military action against German warships turned into a massacre of innocent civilians.

Thursday 3 May opened to skies that were overcast and misty. The weather made visibility difficult but by the afternoon the skies had cleared, revealing an RAF squadron of Hawker Typhoon fighter-bombers preparing to attack German ships in Lübeck bay. Reconnaissance aircraft had already identified several ships berthed in the harbour.

Four Typhoons began the assault on the German shipping. Their first target was the passenger liner *Deutschland*, which was being converted to a hospital ship. It had a crew of eight sailors and a medical staff of 26. Four bombs were launched against it, three of which exploded, but the medical staff managed to escape.

The second attack took place three hours later. Nine Typhoons attacked two more ships, the *Thielbeck* and the *Cap Arcona*. Forty rockets struck the *Cap Arcona* and 30 landed on the smaller ship. Both were sunk with heavy loss of life.

Next day British troops entered Lübeck. Only then did they realize the truth about the previous day's attack. It was not German troops who had fallen victim to their bombs, but thousands of concentration camp inmates.

Around 4,500 of them were on the passenger liner *Cap Arcona*, in addition to 500 SS guards. One of the 350 or so prisoners who had survived described the events of the previous day:

> *On the morning of 3 May there was a terrible explosion. Everyone who could move got very excited and tried to get to the one exit. We felt the ship starting to move fast. Then it stopped. Nobody spoke for an hour.*

Over 4,000 prisoners died on the *Cap Arcona* but most of the SS guards managed to swim to safety. On the *Thielbeck,* only 50 survived out of 2,750. None of the prisoners on board the barges near the ships survived.

The third ship, the *Athen,* was loaded with supplies of rice, flour, macaroni and sugar. Curiously, the quantity of food carried by the ship was far in excess of the needs of all three vessels. Who was the food intended for? Is it possible that the SS were planning to keep the inmates alive and use them as bargaining chips?

In the 1980s, conspiracy theories about the sinking of the *Cap Arcona* appeared in the West German media. One suggested that British intelligence knew that concentration camp inmates were on the vessels but failed to inform the RAF. Another claim was that the RAF knew who was on board but deliberately attacked them to give inexperienced pilots combat training. Yet another conspiracy theory is that the Nazis hoped that the RAF would sink the ships to avoid the SS having to murder the prisoners.

None of the conspiracy theories is remotely plausible. The RAF had strict orders not to bomb ships bearing Red Cross insignia, but in its absence any vessel was a legitimate target. The reaction of the Allies when they entered Lübeck also shows how horrified they were that their bombers had killed innocent victims.

It remains unclear why the *Athen* was laden with such large quantities of supplies. The sinking of the *Cap Arcona,* by contrast, was a human tragedy for which the RAF bombers perhaps cannot reasonably be held responsible.

CHAPTER NINE

MYSTERIES OF THE AIR

DID THE GERMANS FLY TO NEW YORK AND MICHIGAN?

According to some accounts a Junkers Ju-390 left Norway on 27 August 1943 and flew all the way to North America on a reconnaissance mission. Its co-pilot was said to be Anna Kreisling, nicknamed 'The White Wolf of the Luftwaffe' because of her blond hair and piercing blue eyes.

Nine hours after its take-off the plane was reputedly over Canada. It took aerial photographs of industrial sites in Michigan before flying back via New York City. At that point, the USAF detected its presence and chased after it, but the German plane disappeared into the Atlantic Ocean before returning to Paris and landing safely at a nearby airfield.

Kreisling is said to have been a test pilot, flying Junkers Ju-52 Trimotors, the Horton V-9 flying wing and the Ju-390. She is also alleged to have flown in combat missions over Stalingrad. On one occasion, it is said her plane was damaged by Russian fire, but she managed to land safely on a single engine.

The story of this flight has been heavily criticized as mythical and a number of arguments have been put forward against the idea of such a journey.

Did Anna Kreisling exist?

The most cogent of these is the claim that Anna Kreisling was the pilot. Unlike in the Soviet Union, women were not allowed to fly in combat in Nazi Germany. If Kreisling had really fought against Russian planes, it would have made her an internationally known figure and she would have been saluted as a heroine by the Nazis, yet there is no record of her ever having been a pilot.

There were two female test pilots during the Nazi regime; Hanna Reitsch and Melitta von Stauffenberg. In March 1945 Hitler issued an order allowing Reitsch to create a women-only jet fighter squadron, but ten days later, to the intense disappointment of Reitsch, he revoked that order. It is clear from this that German women *never* flew in combat at any stage of the war, so the whole story of Kreisling battling the Soviets at Stalingrad is simply untrue. The lack of any documentary evidence for Kreisling's career as a test pilot – let alone a fighter pilot – makes the story all but impossible to swallow. Further objections to the flight's possibility are based on the capabilities of the Ju-390. It is claimed that it could not have completed its 18,000-mile (29,000 km) journey without refuelling. Perhaps it might just have managed to reach Newfoundland, but no further.

More objections to the veracity of the flight are based on the fact that more than one version of the story exists. In one, the plane takes off on 27 August 1943 and flies from Norway to Michigan and New York. Another dates it to January 1944 and has the aircraft taking off from Mont-de-Marsan near Bordeaux in France and only flying to New York. No mention is made of photographing factories in Michigan.

Another objection is that the source of the Anna Kreisling story is a single writer, Jim Newsom. That may be true in terms of her alleged role in the mission, but Newsom did not invent the idea of a transatlantic flight out of whole cloth.

Public reports of a flight

The first public account of a German flight to America appeared in *RAF Flying Review* for November 1955. That issue included a claim that two Ju-390s had flown to the USA and hovered above New York City for an hour. Then in March 1956 an RAF officer wrote to the magazine with testimony supporting the possibility of the flight.

In June 1944, British intelligence was told by some German prisoners of war that a Ju-390 had flown on a reconnaissance mission to just north of New York City. Two reports from August 1944 stated that the POWs told them that the Ju-390s had photographed the coast of Long Island.

Another source for the story is an article in *Air Progress* for November/December 1965. This mentions the Ju-390 flying over Michigan and New York City. The aviation writer and former editor of *RAF Flying Review*, William Green, repeated the story of the transatlantic flight in his books *Warplanes of the Second World War* and *Warplanes of the Third Reich*.

A report by the US Ninth Air Force dated 1945 described how a captured German photographic technician claimed that a Ju-390 flew from Mont-de-Marsan to within 12 miles (19 km) of New York City. He declared that it photographed the skyline of New York. Another Luftwaffe officer confirmed the story and stated that the Ju-390 was capable of flying for 32 hours without refuelling.

Was the flight possible?

The history of the Ju-390 is not entirely clear. Most aviation historians regard the aircraft's first test flight as being either in August 1943 or in October of the same year. However, both dates make the Kreisling mission look extremely unlikely.

Another suggested date for the flight is January 1944. This date is perhaps more plausible than either August or October 1943.

It has been claimed that the aircraft could not have made the round trip to America as such a journey was beyond its fuel capacity. This objection does not hold up since the aircraft was capable of travelling for twice the distance claimed without refuelling.

The number of Ju-390s that were built is also disputed. The general consensus has been that only two aircraft were ever developed but Kreisling, according to Newsom, said that 11 were built. However, the aviation historian Manfred Griehl has discovered from German archives that seven Ju-390s had been built by June 1944 and that, by May 1944, the Luftwaffe had placed orders for 111 Ju-390s.

In the 1970s, Albert Speer told the author James P. O'Donnell that a Ju-390 flew to Japan in 1944. If that was true, the distance covered by the plane would have been similar to that of the New York flight and confirms that an aerial reconnaissance trip to the East Coast of America was within its range.

Further evidence for a transatlantic flight comes from the wreck of a crashed aircraft in the sea, near Owl's Head Lighthouse, Maine. On 28 September 1944, the US Coastguard found three bodies in the sea and took them to Rockland Maine station. The plane was described by witnesses as being large with six engines and painted in dark green and black. One of the bodies was wearing the uniform of the Luftwaffe Signal Corps, with collar tabs indicating that his rank was Hauptmann (Captain).

Soon after this discovery the area was awash with FBI, military intelligence and other security personnel. They told locals – some of whom had witnessed the plane crashing – that they had seen a German submarine. Later they told them to forget about the entire sighting.

Some years later a diver recovered a constructor's plate from the plane. It was clearly labelled in German and was from the Junkers factory. The only Junkers aircraft with the capacity to fly to Maine in 1944 was the Ju-390.

The flight was certainly possible. Intelligence reports from the time confirm that at least one Ju-390 flew to America and the wreckage off the coast of Maine strongly suggests that at least two flights occurred. If there is the remotest truth in the Anna Kreisling story, at least three Ju-390s flew to the United States during the war.

THE GHOST FIGHTER PLANE OF PEARL HARBOR

The story of the 'ghost fighter of Pearl Harbor' has been around for many years and is often listed as one of the 'strangest unsolved World War II mysteries' on internet sites.

According to the accounts, US radar detected an aircraft heading towards Pearl Harbor from Japan on 8 December 1942. Two fighter planes were sent to intercept the intruder. They saw it was a pre-war P-40 fighter of the type that had been used to defend Pearl Harbor the previous year but had not seen action since. It was missing its landing gear and bore the signs of bullet marks. The pilot lay slumped forward across the controls and seemed to be covered in blood. He then waved at the interceptor planes before nose-diving abruptly and crashing. When the wreckage was examined there was no sign of the pilot, but they discovered a diary stating that the aircraft had been stationed on Mindanao, over 1,000 miles (1,600 km) away.

What happened to the pilot? How did his plane land or take off without landing gear? If the plane had been shot down a year earlier how had the pilot survived and where? Did he repair his aircraft sufficiently to try and return to base?

All of these questions have been asked by people speculating about how it was possible for the pilot to make such an extraordinary flight. The most popular theory is that the pilot somehow scavenged parts to rebuild his wrecked plane but without landing gear had to improvise his return journey.

The 'ghost P-40' certainly seems to be a baffling mystery. Unfortunately, though the story has been repeated on various internet sites and even in a book, it is not true.

Colonel Robert Lee Scott was one of the top American 'aces' in the Pacific War. His 1943 autobiography, *God is My Co-Pilot*, was turned into a film in 1945. In the same year that his life story was filmed by Hollywood, Scott published his second book. It was a collection of short stories called *Damned to Glory*.

The first story in the book, 'Ghost Pilot', gives essentially the same account as the 'unsolved mystery' legend. In 'Ghost Pilot' two airmen called Hampshire and Costello are scrambled from their base in China to intercept a P-40. They are stunned to see it with pre-war insignia on the side and the complete absence of landing gear. Scott wrote:

> *The cockpit had been nearly shot away, the fuselage was a sieve, the right aileron was gone, and one wing seemed shorter than the other where a part of it had been blasted off. Then, as Hampshire moved close beneath the unknown plane, he observed that it had no wheels. The deep wells into which the wheels are supposed to fit when retracted were empty. Enemy bullets couldn't have done that. It had never had wheels.*

The two airmen saw that the pilot was dead, with his head slumped forward over the cockpit. They landed where his plane had crashed and burned and recovered his diary. Within its pages, the dead pilot, Sherrill, describes how he and a small number of Americans found themselves at an airstrip on Mindanao in the Philippines. Everything had been destroyed but the Americans scavenged parts of plane wreckage and built a reasonably functional P-40. However, they were unable to salvage any landing gear.

They then came up with the idea of using bamboo skids for their take-off. Once they were airborne, they jettisoned them. Loading the plane with bombs, they planned to attack Japanese-held Formosa (now Taiwan) and then fly to the American base in China.

Sherrill flew slowly and managed to drop his bomb-load on to the Japanese base. During his raid he was mortally wounded, but he managed to fly back almost as far as his original USAF base in China.

The only significant difference between Scott's story and the 'unsolved mystery' is the location of the events, with the pilot returning to Pearl Harbor rather than China. This perhaps came about because the P-40 in the stories is described as being pre-war. The insignia on a P-40 on 7 December 1941, the date of the Pearl Harbor attack, would have been pre-war (pre-war in this case meaning before the US entered the war). That is, a white star filled with a red dot on a navy-blue circle. After 11 May 1942, the red dot was dropped to avoid confusion with the 'rising sun' insignia used by the Japanese.

Scott's story is fascinating but perhaps the real mystery is how so many internet sites and even some authors have recycled a gripping yarn into sober fact.

WHY WERE RUSSIAN PILOTS IN SCOTLAND?

During World War II a group of Soviet pilots were stationed in Scotland between 1943 and 1944. They were being trained to fly Albemarle transport aircraft. The pilots belonged to the 1st Air Transportation Division of the Soviet Civil Air Fleet.

There was a shortage of suitable transport aircraft in Russia and by summer 1942 this was making it difficult for the Soviets to deploy troops quickly. In September 1942, Ivan Maisky, the Soviet ambassador to the UK, made a formal request to the British government for help. The British responded by offering the Russians 100 Albemarle twin-engined planes that had been originally designed for use as bombers. Commissioned in 1938, the Albemarle's fuselage and central wing consisted of a tubular steel frame with a plywood covering. Once production began, it was discovered that the plane was unsuitable for use as a bomber and it was therefore redeployed as a transport aircraft.

The planes were transferred to the Soviet Union, flying from Prestwick in Scotland and across Norway, Sweden and the Baltic Sea to Moscow. As well as the planes, the government offered to train Russian crews on the Albemarles in Scotland. Twenty crews were formed in the 1st Air Transportation Division and the first group of them came to Scotland on 11 January 1943.

They were based at RAF Errol aerodrome, where a number of Allied countries sent their pilots for training. Two thousand staff were stationed there.

The Russian pilots and flight engineers studied the Albemarle aircraft at the factories and the aerodrome. However, the head of the Soviet Military Mission soon identified some problems. A report by Admiral Nikolai Kharlamov explained that 'a considerable drawback is our airmen's appearance as they arrived in varying uniforms and without insignia. That complicated communication between them and the British instructor-officers, as the latter consider our pilots to be of low rank.' As a result of this confusion, from then onwards uniforms for the aircrews were ordered from a tailor in Dundee.

Over the next two months, seven further groups arrived in Scotland. After being trained on the Albemarles at RAF Errol, they then flew the first consignment of the planes back to the Soviet Union. Britain also promised to provide the Russians with another 100 Albemarles.

On 3 March, the first Albemarle flew from Britain and landed at Vnukovo airfield, after a journey of 11 and a quarter hours. By the end of April, 14 Albemarles had been flown out of Scotland but two failed to reach Vnukovo. One was simply reported as missing and another was shot down by German anti-aircraft fire.

During a training flight, an Albemarle crashed near Loch Tay. The eyewitnesses testified how the crew managed to steer the aircraft away from the nearby houses and avoid civilian casualties. Unfortunately, though, they could not save their own lives.

By June 1943, all of the Russian air crew had been successfully trained at Errol. They also watched Halifax bombers taking off for a raid on Berlin.

The Soviet pilots did not have a high opinion of the Albemarle as an aircraft. They also found a safer route via Fairbanks in Alaska to Krasnoyarsk in Siberia. The Americans then made available the Douglas C-47 aircraft, which was far superior to the Albemarle.

In 2015, a tribute to the Russian pilots was held in Scotland when the Montrose Air Station Heritage Centre held a special exhibition entitled 'The Russians Are Coming'. On 16 May, a commemorative plaque to the Russian pilots was unveiled at the disused Errol airfield.

THE LOST LIBERATOR

On 4 April 1943, the crew of a USAAF B-24D Liberator went on the aircraft's first combat mission. It failed to return to base and all of the crew were reported as 'missing in action'. The original theory was that the nine-man crew had crashed into the Mediterranean Sea and that remained the official verdict until the accidental discovery of the wrecked plane in the Libyan desert by oil workers from British Petroleum on 9 November 1958.

Following this unexpected discovery an investigation into the crash was launched. It came to the conclusion that the crew, who had only arrived in Libya a week earlier and had not flown together before, got lost in a sandstorm and overflew their base.

They flew south into the desert before the aircraft ran low on fuel and at that point they bailed out and tried to walk to safety but perished in the desert.

Two years later, the bodies of all but one of the crew members were found. The aircraft wreckage was moved to a Libyan Air Force base.

The Liberator, with its name *Lady Be Good* hand-painted on the starboard side, was part of a bomber squad based at Soluch Field in Libya. Its mission was to fly to Naples and bomb the harbour as part of an attack by a group of 25 planes.

Misfortune dogged the Liberator from the beginning of its flight. It was one of the last aircraft to leave and almost as soon as it took to the air poor visibility and high winds made it lose contact with the rest of the bombers. Conditions were so bad that nine of the team returned to base, but *Lady Be Good* continued the raid on its own. It arrived successfully at Naples that evening, but poor visibility again made it difficult for the aircraft to see the target clearly.

Flying back alone from Italy, the pilot of *Lady Be Good* radioed to tell the base that his automatic direction finder did not work properly. He asked the base to give him their location, but the plane overflew it and the desert conditions were so bad that the flares fired by the base to guide the aircraft home could not be seen.

For the next two hours, the plane flew further and further into the Sahara Desert. Eventually the fuel began to run out and the crew parachuted out of the aircraft to the ground. The plane continued on its own for 16 miles (26 km) before crashing. No trace of the aircraft or its crew could be found.

One engine was still operational at the time of the crash and the plane was mainly intact. It must have lost height gradually and landed on its undercarriage in the desert. When the BP team discovered the wreckage, its radio and guns were still in working order and there was even some food and water left on the aircraft. No parachutes were found nor was there any sign of the crew, so it was clear that they had all bailed out of the plane before it crashed.

In February 1960, the bodies of five crew members were found. Later that year, a further three bodies were recovered from the desert sand. Only one of the crew's bodies was never found and it is believed that it was his remains that a British Army patrol recovered and buried in 1953, unaware that there were any Allied airmen listed as missing in that area.

The co-pilot kept a diary as the crew tried to walk northwards out of the desert. None of them knew where they were when they bailed out. They managed to exist for eight days in the desert with only one canteen of water between them, but eventually they split up, with five staying behind while three went off to seek help. Sadly, none of them survived and the diary found on the co-pilot's body tells a story of courage and increasing desperation as they realized that they were not going to live.

Wheelus Air Base has a stained-glass window commemorating *Lady Be Good* and her brave but doomed crew members.

WHO SHOT DOWN DOUGLAS BADER?

Douglas Bader was one of the most famous RAF pilots during World War II. He has been credited with 22 victories, six probable victories and four shared victories and he also damaged a total of 11 German aircraft.

He joined the RAF in 1928 and was commissioned two years later. In 1931, he crashed and lost his legs and on his recovery he applied to be returned to flying duties, but his application was refused and he was medically retired. However, on the outbreak of war, he returned to the RAF and was allowed to serve as a pilot. During the retreat from Dunkirk, Bader scored his first aerial victories. He then became heavily involved in the Battle of Britain.

In August 1941, he bailed out over France and was captured, spending the rest of the war as a POW. During his captivity, he made several attempts to escape and was transferred to Colditz Castle, considered escape-proof. Although some prisoners managed to escape from Colditz, Bader was not among them and he was not freed until 1945.

Bader believed that his aircraft had collided in mid-air with a Bf 109 over France. Following the collision, his fin, tail and fuselage were damaged beyond repair and he rapidly began to lose altitude. He initially tried to bail out, but his prosthetic leg prevented that. Eventually, he was able to release his parachute and his leg was pulled free. As he approached the ground, he saw a Bf 109 flying past.

Hands in pockets, Douglas Bader, the famous legless pilot, poses in front of a Hurricane alongside Canadian pilots of 242 Squadron.

German records show that no Bf 109 was involved in a collision, however, and although two German pilots claimed a victory that day neither of their claims corresponds with the details of Bader's crash.

Recent research suggests that Bader, having lost contact with his squadron, may have been shot down by one of his fellow pilots. Flight Lieutenant Casson of 616 Squadron claimed to have shot down a Bf 109 and said he saw its tail become detached and the pilot bailing out. He eventually realized that he must have mistaken Bader's plane for a German aircraft and shot him down by mistake.

Bader's Spitfire has never been found. It is believed to have crashed and this is supported by the testimony of a French eyewitness who saw the plane disintegrating as it approached the ground.

GUY GIBSON: DEATH OF A DAMBUSTER

Wing Commander Guy Gibson was one of the leading pilots in RAF Bomber Command during World War II. By the time of his death at the age of 26, he had completed over 170 flying operations.

Gibson wanted to fly even as a child. His bedroom wall carried a picture of Albert Ball VC, a British flying ace during World War I. He planned to become a test pilot and when he applied to Vickers he was advised to join the RAF. However, when he attempted to enlist he was rejected because his legs were too short. Later he reapplied and this time he was admitted, beginning his career with the RAF in 1936.

By the summer of 1937, he was already displaying a preference for bombers over fighter aircraft. He was also acquiring a reputation for being surly. Technically, he was a good flyer, but his personal skills were not commensurate with his qualities as a pilot. He was particularly censured for behaving rudely towards junior officers and ground crew.

Gibson began his career with 83 (Bomber) Squadron, where he flew Hawker Hinds. He continued to treat the ground staff with disrespect, as he had done at his previous posting, and soon acquired the nickname of the 'Bumptious Bastard'. Then he began to acquire a reputation for recklessness when he was hauled before a Court of Inquiry in October 1938 and was found guilty of negligence. In 1939, 83 Squadron was issued with Handley Page Hampdens, so Gibson had to learn to fly the new aircraft.

Gibson was on leave in the summer of 1939 when he was suddenly recalled on 31 August. He was about to become one of the most famous pilots of World War II.

His first wartime flight was on 3 September 1939, only two days after the declaration of war. He was chosen to attack the German Navy near Wilhelmshaven. Bad weather forced the attempt to be abandoned and he did not fly again until December.

In February 1940, he was part of a squadron sent to attack a U-boat, but communications errors led to one of the planes dropping its bombs on a Royal Navy submarine instead. The officers were given a severe reprimand and ordered to receive intensive training.

Then in April 1940, Gibson entered one of the most hectic periods of his flying career. In five months he completed 34 operations, ten of them in June. His tasks included laying mines, attacking ships and bombing targets on the ground. He built up a reputation as being fearless and happy to fly in poor weather conditions and on 9 July 1940 he received the Distinguished Flying Cross (DFC).

On 13 November 1940, Gibson reported to 29 Squadron and was given command of 'A' flight. The squadron was not very effective and its main aircraft was the Bristol Blenheim, which was unsuitable as a night fighter. There were also too few trained pilots available. In spite of these constraints Gibson flew six operations in the Blenheims.

Once the squadron began flying the Bristol Beaufighter, things improved. Gibson found that night fighting was very different from bombing. The crew had to work as a team and the pilot had to rely on the guidance of the AI operator to identify targets. Gibson was relatively successful though disappointed not to be the leading 'ace' in the squadron. On 15 December, he left and was awarded a bar to his DFC.

After a rest from operations, Gibson decided that he would rather fly bombers. On 22 March 1942, he was summoned for an interview with Air Officer Commander-in-Chief Arthur Harris. He promoted Gibson to wing commander and posted him to 106 Squadron, where he was put in charge of a squadron of Lancasters.

Gibson began by laying mines in the Baltic and soon began bombing operations on a wider scale. He was known to be aggressive, a risk-taker and a stern disciplinarian. At times, this led him to make errors of judgement and he was not popular with many of his crew. His attitude towards ground crew and NCOs continued to attract criticism and before long he acquired a new nickname, 'The Boy Emperor'.

In March 1943, Gibson was selected to lead the RAF's new 617 Squadron, whose task was to destroy dams in the Ruhr valley. Then on 24 March, Gibson met Barnes Wallis for the first time. Wallis explained his new 'bouncing bomb' and a few days later Gibson was told to practise bombing lakes and reservoirs in the Midlands and Wales. On 29 March, he was shown models of the Möhne and Sorpe dams and, on 16–17 May, Gibson was the main participant in the 'Dambusters' raid, when the Möhne, Sorpe and Eder dams were targeted. The bombs breached the Möhne and Eder dams but did virtually no damage to the Sorpe. Eight planes were lost and 56 crew members died during the raid. Gibson was awarded the Victoria Cross for his part in the attack.

Mystery crash

After the raid, Gibson was retired from active flying duty and toured Britain and the United States. He chafed under these restrictions and pleaded to be allowed to fly again. Eventually, the authorities relented, but in September 1944 his Mosquito crashed and Gibson and his navigator failed to survive.

The RAF quickly issued a report on the crash. This stated that there were no aircraft near him when he crashed, so the verdict was that Gibson had either run out of fuel or had been brought down by ground anti-aircraft fire.

Gibson was 26 years old at the time of his death. Already a legend and decorated with the DSO and bar and DFC and bar in addition to his Victoria Cross, his status as a national hero made it essential to tell the public that he had died a hero's death.

The problem is that the official explanation may be false and he might have been killed by a gunner from a Lancaster bomber. For many years, the flight combat reports of Lancaster crew members in the vicinity were classified. When they were finally released into the public domain, a different story emerged.

Sergeant Bernard McCormack was the unfortunate Lancaster gunner who mistook Gibson's Mosquito for a German aircraft. His combat report shows that he was in the area where Gibson was flying and that he had shot at what he believed to be a Ju 88.

Another Lancaster crew was also in the area and reported seeing a Mosquito out of control before it crashed. They said that four red target flares exploded when the plane crashed and those were the same flares carried by Gibson's Mosquito. The flying time and position of both Lancaster combat crews also corresponded to the spot where Gibson's aircraft had crashed.

McCormack was interrogated by an RAF intelligence officer and he later made a tape recording of what he thought had occurred.

> *We were on our way back over Holland and then all of a sudden this kite [aircraft] comes right behind us twin engines and a single rudder – and it comes bouncing in towards us so we opened fire and we blew him up.*

The day after the crew had claimed to have shot down a Ju 88 they were questioned by RAF intelligence. When the officer pointed out to the crew that the Mosquito, like a Ju 88, had twin engines and a single rudder it dawned on McCormack that he had shot down and killed Gibson.

The RAF could not admit to the death of a war hero by friendly fire, so instead it had created two plausible cover stories – running out of fuel and ground anti-aircraft fire. McCormack never spoke of that day again but his tape recording gives his account of the events of that night.

It remains possible that Gibson, who had very little experience of flying Mosquitoes, may have misjudged the amount of fuel left in the tank or simply lost control of the aircraft. The idea of a faulty fuel gauge has also been suggested as a possible cause. Gibson's notorious arrogance may have led him to imagine that he could fly his way out of danger.

On the whole, however, McCormack's account seems the most credible explanation of the death of one of the most gifted pilots of World War II, but the truth will never be known with certainty.

CHAPTER TEN
MYSTERIES OF ESPIONAGE

WAS PEARL HARBOR A SURPRISE ATTACK?

On 7 December 1941, the Japanese attacked the United States Pacific fleet at Pearl Harbor in Hawaii. Ever since there has been disagreement over whether or not this attack was really a surprise to the US. Was it simply the result of incompetence and complacency by the Americans or a cynical conspiracy by the US government and/or other Allied nations to drag the United States into the war at the expense of the lives of American sailors? Before examining this question, it is necessary to examine the background to events before the Japanese attack.

There is no doubt that from the outbreak of war in September 1939 President Roosevelt was entirely sympathetic to the Allies. He feared and disliked Nazism and if the domestic political climate had been more favourable he might well have intervened earlier.

Nevertheless, Roosevelt had full control of the Democratic Party and was able to persuade it to support a number of measures that were dubiously legal in view of the United States' professed neutrality.

Isolationist sentiment was strong in the United States, but it was not nearly as powerful as is sometimes claimed. Some groups, particularly German Americans and to a lesser extent some Irish Americans, were hostile towards Britain and at least sympathetic to the Nazis, but that was a minority view. Most Americans, however much they may have wished to stay outside the conflict, were broadly supportive of the Allies.

This is shown most clearly through the surprising choice by the Republicans of Wendell Willkie as their candidate in the 1940 presidential election. Willkie, a former Democrat and a businessman, won his way to the nomination in the teeth of opposition from the Republican establishment. He was a strong champion of intervention in the 'European war' and his anti-isolationist sentiments were clearly popular enough for him to become the Republican nominee.

Willkie's nomination also gave Roosevelt greater breathing space and more confidence that the US could somehow be brought into the war. If the Republicans had picked one of the isolationist candidates, his task might have been more difficult. Roosevelt was running for an unprecedented (and unique) third term in office and Willkie's candidature meant that both parties were broadly in support of a more overtly anti-Nazi policy.

When Roosevelt was re-elected, Willkie continued to support a policy of intervention. This enabled the president to push through measures that would have been far more difficult without bipartisan support.

Caught unprepared, US forces took a pasting when the Japanese attacked Pearl Harbor in 1941. But did the attack come as a surprise to the US government?

Did Roosevelt provoke the attack?

Relations between the US and Japan had been poor for many years. From 1937 onwards, the Japanese had engaged in a bloody war with China, in the course of which they committed numerous atrocities. America was aware that Japan was dominated by a military regime and that it had its eyes on conquering large parts of Asia. The Dutch East Indies and British colonies in Malaya, Singapore, Hong Kong and elsewhere were all viewed as possible additions to the Japanese Empire. The Philippines was a particular concern to the United States as its proximity to Japan and its relative lack of defensive capability made it an easy target. US military and foreign affairs specialists considered a Japanese attack on the Philippines to be the most likely target in the event of war.

Roosevelt froze Japanese assets in the US, reduced and eventually halted exports to Japan, closed the Panama Canal to Japanese ships and issued a threat of force if Japan did not abandon its militaristic ambitions in the Pacific. With the outbreak of war in Europe, he adopted an increasingly bellicose tone towards the Japanese and eventually these steps, particularly the restrictions on raw materials, led to Japan attacking the United States.

One reason the American public had been reluctant to become directly involved in the European conflict was the memory of the four-year stalemate on the Western Front. In 1939, the Phoney War made people on both sides of the Atlantic wonder if a negotiated peace could be obtained.

These illusions vanished with the blitzkrieg that saw German troops sweeping through Holland and Belgium and into France. The British Army had to beat a humiliating retreat at Dunkirk and the French were forced to surrender. Suddenly Germany was the master of western Europe and Britain found itself facing a victorious enemy with only the English Channel and the Royal Air Force to defend it.

The unexpected dominance of Germany in Europe changed American perceptions. Sympathy for Britain grew as the Battle of Britain saw outnumbered RAF pilots fighting and defeating the Luftwaffe. The effect on American public opinion of the Blitz was even more pronounced. Unlike Joseph Kennedy, most Americans began to admire Britain's resolve and courage and saw that Germany could be beaten.

It is also true that while Europe might have played a less than prominent part in American thinking the alleged isolationism of the US is sharply refuted by an opinion poll from the era. This showed that a large majority of the population were concerned about Japanese activities in the Pacific and favoured war with Japan. Willkie's nomination by the Republicans is further proof that the degree of support for isolationist policies in the US was far smaller than generally believed.

There is no doubt that Roosevelt set out to provoke the Japanese, but how far he was simply playing a game of brinkmanship and how far he intended war is more questionable. He had frozen German assets in the United States, depth-charged U-boats in American waters and sent 50 destroyers to Britain, all actions in clear violation of neutrality, but the Germans had simply failed to respond. It was quite possible that the Japanese would have followed the Nazi example.

Realistically, the Japanese can hardly have expected to defeat the United States in war. As events showed it was certainly possible for them to conquer British, French and Dutch possessions, but beating America was in a different order of magnitude.

Pearl Harbor was certainly vulnerable to attack. In 1940, the Pacific Fleet commander, Admiral Richardson, had flown to

Washington to ask Roosevelt to move its base from Hawaii to the West Coast. He pointed out that it could be approached from any point of the compass, it was difficult for him to train and supply crews, it was impossible to defend it adequately against torpedo attacks and the morale of men at considerable distance from their families was also affected. Richardson said later that: 'I came away with the impression that, despite his spoken word, the President was fully determined to put the United States into the war if Great Britain could hold out until he was re-elected.'

Apparently the exchanges between the two men grew heated and Richardson was dismissed by Roosevelt. He was replaced by Admiral Kimmel. Kimmel quickly told Roosevelt of the problems at Pearl Harbor, but his doubts were overcome.

There are three versions of the conspiracy theory surrounding the attack on Pearl Harbor. One claims that Churchill warned Roosevelt of the forthcoming Japanese assault but that both leaders remained silent. A second claims that Churchill knew of the coming attack, but kept the truth from Roosevelt. The third claims that Roosevelt deliberately planned to provoke the Japanese into attacking Pearl Harbor and sacrificed the Pacific Fleet and the lives of its men to bring America into the war.

All have some degree of plausibility, but all are open to serious objections. Before dealing with the specific claims, it is worth remembering that historians too often look at Pearl Harbor simply from the point of view of the Americans. The Japanese had been militarily active in the Pacific for years and during that time they had extensively studied American naval dispositions and had maps and technical specifications. The extent to which the Japanese had been planning for a potential war against the United States has been too easily forgotten in the furore over culpability for Pearl Harbor.

The Pearl Harbor attack

The attack on Pearl Harbor had been planned in meticulous detail by Admiral Yamamoto. He had lived and worked in the United States and spoke fluent English. Yamamoto read two books written by the British intelligence officer Hector Bywater. One was entitled *Sea-Power in the Pacific*. Though it was published in 1925, it was widely known and had been translated into Japanese.

Bywater's book predicted a surprise attack on Pearl Harbor. It then imagined an encounter between the Japanese and American fleets in the Philippines. Bywater predicted that aircraft carriers would play a decisive role in the battle and his book also foretold Japanese attacks on Guam and the Philippines with massive bombardment by sea and air before Japanese troops invaded.

Not only did Yamamoto speak and read English but the availability of a Japanese translation makes it even more probable that he read Bywater. As early as 1927, he had taken part in 'war games', including an attack on Pearl Harbor and, in December 1940, he began making preparations for the forthcoming attack.

It took him eight months to persuade the Japanese naval staff that his risky plan was viable. As late as 24 September 1941, it was rejected as being too dangerous.

Faced with this opposition, Yamamoto pulled rank. By now he was commander-in-chief of the navy and was able to insist that planning for the attack must go ahead. He then confronted the navy minister and gave him an ultimatum. Unless the plan was approved, he would resign. He added that the senior officers of the fleet would follow his example.

This precipitated a crisis within the Japanese government. Most of them had become convinced that war with America was inevitable and that some kind of pre-emptive strike offered the best opportunity to maximize their chances of success.

The plan to attack Pearl Harbor was further strengthened by the series of reconnaissance flights that had been made from Taiwan since April 1941. The Philippines, Guam and a number of other US bases were photographed and agents also passed on information.

Once he was armed with all the data necessary for the attack, Yamamoto ordered the fleet and air force to move off and assault Pearl Harbor. The task force set off on 26 November under the command of Vice-Admiral Chuichi Nagumo. This appointment turned out to be a mistake, though at first the mission was completely successful.

The fleet took the longer northern route to Hawaii to reduce the chances of being detected, maintaining perfect radio silence until it was 200 miles (320 km) north of Hawaii. At that point, it received the message 'Climb Mount Fujiyama', which was the coded signal to begin the assault.

On 7 December hundreds of Japanese aircraft flew from their aircraft carriers, reaching their target in just under two hours. At 7.49 a.m., the attack began. Bombs and torpedoes hammered the US Pacific fleet and by 10 a.m. eight American ships had been destroyed or put out of action. Air force bases were also pounded, with 163 planes being wrecked and a further 159 damaged.

At that point, caution overcame Nagumo and he refused to carry out a third attack as Yamamoto's plan had required. This meant that the oil bunkers on Hawaii and other important military targets were not devastated or damaged.

Pearl Harbor, in spite of Nagumo's failure to completely destroy US capability in the region, was a stunning military triumph for the Japanese. It emboldened them to begin their attack on a variety of nations in Asia with, initially at least, rapid success.

Conspiracy theories examined

Ever since that day conspiracy theories have proliferated. Yamamoto's detailed knowledge of the area and the disposition of the fleet was at first put down to Allied treachery. In fact, it was the result of years of careful research and planning, which also explained his ability to strike at the target swiftly and unerringly. What is more arguable is the extent to which the Allied nations knew of the Japanese plans.

At its most extreme, some have claimed that Roosevelt deliberately sacrificed the Pacific Fleet to bring America into the war. Those who urge this theory point out that the US had cracked the Japanese secret code known as 'Purple' in 1940. Several copies of the decoding machine were made, but none were sent to Pearl Harbor.

After that, other information gradually came to light. As early as 27 January 1941, the US ambassador to Japan sent a message to the government reporting what he had heard from a Peruvian minister. The message stated: 'In the event of trouble breaking out between the United States and Japan, the Japanese intended to make a surprise attack against Pearl Harbor with all their strength.'

Then in summer 1941 Dusko Popov, a Yugoslav double agent who pretended to be a German agent but was secretly working for the Allies, was asked by the Germans to go to Hawaii and make a detailed study of Pearl Harbor and its defences. He reported this information to the FBI in New York. J. Edgar Hoover later claimed that he had passed on this warning to Roosevelt but that the president had told him not to take the matter any further.

Hoover's claim is open to doubt on two grounds. In the first place, there are counter-claims that he knew of Pearl Harbor independently but chose not to inform the president. Secondly, his own version of events surfaced much later and was almost certainly intended to justify himself and deflect criticism from the FBI.

On 9 October 1941, a message from Tokyo to the Japanese consul-general in Hawaii was decoded. It ordered him to divide Pearl Harbor into five areas and report the locations of US ships in the harbour. The logical interpretation of this message is that an attack on Pearl Harbor was planned by the Japanese and might be imminent.

In December 1941, the Dutch decoded a Japanese dispatch to the embassy in Bangkok, which predicted attacks on four targets including Hawaii. This was passed on to the US military observer in the region and the Dutch military attaché in Washington also warned General George Marshall of the decrypted information.

There are also conflicting claims that the Soviet spy Richard Sorge knew about Pearl Harbor and warned Stalin. One version claims that Stalin passed the information on to Roosevelt and the other version claims that he did not. Neither claim has ever been substantiated.

There is no doubt that Roosevelt wanted to bring America into the war. It is also certain that Japanese aggression in Asia had alarmed both the government and US public opinion. From 1937 onwards, a deliberate campaign of economic and other sanctions against Japan had made it more difficult for the Japanese to continue their warlike policies. It is clear from various statements by senior US government figures that the prospect of war with Japan was seen as highly probable, just as it is clear that public opinion would have overwhelmingly supported a war against the Japanese.

On the other hand, it is also plain on the basis of government documents that while the prospect of a Japanese attack was considered likely it was believed that the 'first strike' in such an assault would be directed against the Philippines. There is no convincing evidence that the US government imagined that Pearl Harbor would be a target for Japan. They may even have known that senior Japanese ministers and naval commanders considered such an attack to be too risky to undertake.

It is highly probable that the American military and political establishment were too complacent about the prospect of an assault on Pearl Harbor. Complacency and incompetence are more likely explanations for the lackadaisical American attitude than conscious treason.

There is also the further complication that if Roosevelt provoked an attack on Pearl Harbor he would be taking a huge risk that the attack might backfire on him. History was not on his side, nor was sober calculation. When Hitler found himself at war with Britain and France, neither Japan nor, at first, Italy, joined him. There was no reason, therefore, to assume that war between Japan and the United States would extend beyond a conflict between those two nations. He could not have known that Hitler, already heavily committed in the Soviet Union, would make the mistake of declaring war on the US after Pearl Harbor. Germany could have remained neutral, which would have forced America to concentrate its resources purely on a Pacific war and make the task of liberating Europe far more difficult. To sacrifice the Pacific Fleet on the off-chance that Hitler might be foolish enough to declare war on the United States was too great a gamble. Roosevelt and his team were certainly complacent, but they were not stupid. The idea that the US government deliberately chose to sacrifice Pearl Harbor to achieve American entry into the war is simply implausible and is contradicted by the available evidence.

Two key planks in the conspiracy theory have both been shown to be false. One is that the US had intercepted Japanese radio messages, which is simply not true as the fleet maintained complete radio silence. The other concerns an alleged telegram from Churchill to Roosevelt warning the US of an imminent Japanese attack on Pearl Harbor.

There are two versions of the 'Churchill' conspiracy theory. One maintains that Churchill knew of the coming assault but withheld the information from Roosevelt. This cannot be disproved but it is highly improbable.

The other version claims that Churchill sent a telegram to Roosevelt warning of the forthcoming attack. This is a fabrication with no substance. Churchill did send Roosevelt a telegram on 26 November 1941, but it expressed his concern about events in China, where the Japanese were having marked success against the Chinese.

Conspiracy theorists make much of the fact that a 'secret file' was withheld from the public domain for years. When it was eventually released it turned out to relate to the treasonable actions of a Scottish peer who had leaked information to the Japanese.

The whole notion of a conspiracy by Churchill and/or Roosevelt is therefore dead in the water. There is no evidence to support it and plenty of contrary facts that show it is simply false.

THE MECHELEN INCIDENT

The Mechelen Incident is the name given to an event that took place on 10 January 1940 when a German plane crashed near Vucht in Belgium. The pilot, Erich Hoenmanns, was accompanied by a passenger, Helmuth Reinberger. Unknown to Hoenmanns, Reinberger was carrying top secret documents relating to *Fall Gelb* (Case Yellow), the Nazi plans for the forthcoming attack on Holland and Belgium. At the time of the crash, this was scheduled to take place on 17 January.

When the plane crashed, the two-man crew had no idea of their location. The pilot asked a nearby farm labourer where they were and was horrified when he was told that they were now in Belgium. Reinberger was even more agitated and rushed back to the plane in search of his briefcase. He foolishly told Hoenmanns that he had top secret documents in the case that he urgently needed to destroy and this was overheard by the farmhand. While Reinberger was unsuccessfully trying to burn the documents with his cigarette lighter, Hoenmanns tried to move away from the plane to divert attention from what his passenger was doing. Frantic at his failure to burn the documents, Reinberger went over to the farm labourer and asked for a match. He then went behind a thicket and piled up the documents on the ground and tried to burn them.

The commotion attracted the attention of two border guards, who rushed across and stopped him after seeing the smoke. Reinberger tried to flee but was captured after the guards had fired two warning shots.

Documents seized

The guards took the two Germans prisoner and they were held at the border guardhouse near Mechelen-aan-de-Maas. A Belgian military intelligence officer then interrogated them, placing the partly burned documents on the table in front of them. Hoenmanns, warned by Reinberger of the paramount importance of the material he was carrying, tried to create a diversion by asking to use the toilet. As he was doing so, Reinberger seized the papers and tried to burn them in a nearby stove. He managed to put them in the stove, but burned his hand when he picked up the hot lid. The startled officer snatched the papers out of the stove, burning his own hand in the process. Following this, he removed the documents and moved them to another room, which was locked.

Reinberger then realized that all was lost. He knew that he had allowed the plans for the invasion of Holland and Belgium to fall into enemy hands. At that point, he tried to grab the officer's gun but was knocked down. Crying uncontrollably, Reinberger remonstrated with his captor.

'I wanted your revolver to kill myself.'

Hoenmanns then turned to the Belgian officer and added: 'He's finished now.'

Two hours passed before regular Belgian intelligence officers arrived. They took the papers away and passed them on to their superior later that afternoon.

The news of the crashed plane reached Berlin in the late evening. It caused utter alarm in the German High Command, who realized that Reinberger had been carrying with him details of the planned invasion of the Low Countries. The following day Hitler, infuriated at the news, fired two senior military officers.

A heated discussion then ensued about whether or not to abandon, or at least modify, the plans in light of the fact that the details of the original attack schedule were now in the hands of Belgium and, probably, Holland. German military attachés in the Netherlands and Belgium were asked to investigate how far the loss of the plans had compromised the original scheme.

Two days later, General Alfred Jodl, chief of operations for the Wehrmacht, reported to Hitler that 'if the enemy is in possession of all the files, situation catastrophic'. This pessimistic assessment was soon altered by a campaign of deliberate deception on the part of Belgian intelligence.

Belgian deception campaign

The first ploy by the Belgians was attempting to deceive Reinberger into believing that he had succeeded in destroying the papers.

Initially they asked him what the plans contained and warned him that if he refused to answer he would be treated as a spy rather than as an officer. Reinberger, testifying later, said that:

> *From the way this question was asked, I realized that he [the intelligence officer interrogating him] could not have understood anything from the fragments of the documents he had seen.*

The second ploy was to allow Hoenmanns and Reinberger to meet German military attachés while secretly recording their conversations. During this meeting Reinberger told them that he thought he had managed to destroy the papers sufficiently to make them illegible. This statement seemed to be successful and following the meeting the news was passed on to the German ambassador to Belgium. He in turn sent a telegram to the German authorities stating that:

> *Major Reinberger has confirmed that he burned the documents except for some pieces which are the size of the palm of his hand. Reinberger confirms that most of the documents which could not be destroyed appear to be unimportant.*

Satisfied with this information, Jodl reported that: 'Despatch case burnt for certain.'

Meanwhile, the Belgian authorities were busy analysing the documents. Although the truth was that Reinberger had managed to destroy much of their contents, enough remained to make it clear that the plans involved a German invasion of Holland and Belgium. There was no indication of the proposed date of the attack but from the reaction of Reinberger it was deduced that it would be imminent.

On 11 January, General Raoul Van Overstraeten decided that the information in the plans was an accurate account of a forthcoming German invasion. He informed the king who in turn told the minister of defence and the French commander-in-chief, General Maurice Gamelin. The commander of the British Expeditionary Force, Lord Gort, was also given a warning that plans for a German attack on Holland and Belgium had been discovered. King Leopold then personally informed Princess Juliana of Holland and the Grand Duchess of Luxembourg of the imminent danger.

Gamelin was not only convinced of the genuineness of the information – a view not shared by all of the French High Command – but he hoped it could be used to put pressure on the Dutch and the Belgians to allow French troops to move into their countries and use them as secure bases for an invasion of Germany. He also believed that the clear evidence of German intentions to violate the neutrality of Holland and Belgium might make them more willing to allow the Allies to pass through their countries.

Meanwhile, the Belgian military attaché in Berlin forwarded a warning to his government. He announced that he had received information from a 'sincere informer' – now known to have been the anti-Nazi officer Colonel Hans Oster – that 'the attack will happen tomorrow to pre-empt countermeasures'.

At that point, doubts crept into Belgian thinking. Van Overstraeten was amazed that the informant knew about the plans, which had not been made public. Was it some elaborate German deception to mislead them into acting hastily? However, in spite of his doubts, he issued a warning that an attack was imminent and a Belgian military commander then issued orders cancelling leave for the armed forces.

Neither the king nor Van Overstraeten knew of this move and

were furious at the decision. The offending officer resigned at the end of the month in disgrace.

The Dutch, unlike the Belgians, never took the information seriously. They cancelled leave for Dutch troops, but otherwise did not respond.

German change of plan

Meanwhile, the Germans were busy considering the consequences of the crash. Even though they believed that the plans were unreadable, Jodl still became concerned, particularly as there were clear signs of activity by the French and the Belgians. The weather also deteriorated, with heavy snowfall making an invasion more difficult. At that point, Jodl advised Hitler to postpone the plan and he reluctantly agreed.

After the abandonment of the original plans for the attack, a radical rethinking of the strategy ensued. There is some disagreement about whether or not this would have occurred without the loss of the plans at Mechelen.

Hitler had always had reservations about the original plan. He believed it was too predictable and old-fashioned and that a more dynamic approach was necessary. Although he had been willing to concur with the Mechelen plans, he had always felt that an approach based on surprise and a shorter phase of attack was more likely to achieve results.

General Erich von Manstein had long been sceptical about the original plan. He had been championing a different strategy for some months, involving concentrating German tanks further to the south. On 13 February, Hitler agreed, telling Jodl:

> *We should attack in the direction of Sedan. The enemy is not expecting us to attack there. The documents held by the*

Luftwaffe officers who crash landed have convinced the enemy that we only intend to take over the Dutch and Belgian coasts.

A few days later, Hitler formally approved von Manstein's plan. It allowed the Germans to lay a trap for the Allies, who still imagined that the Germans would follow the path of invasion laid down in the documents captured at Mechelen. The result was that the French and British forces were caught by surprise when the invasion eventually occurred. Their lack of flexibility led to a catastrophic military defeat. In spite of these facts, it is not the case that the original plans that were lost when the plane crashed were deliberate disinformation. What happened is that the Germans adapted to the new situation and pretended that the original plan of attack still stood. The Mechelen Incident was an accident rather than a devious ploy by the Nazis to mislead the Allies.

THE 'LUCY' SPY RING

The 'Lucy' spy ring was one of the most effective anti-Nazi intelligence networks during World War II. It was based in Switzerland and its leader worked for several intelligence networks. Originally, the ring analysed data from Swiss military intelligence, but it soon began working with anti-Nazi German officers.

Some of this data was passed on by Swiss military intelligence to MI6. Later the Russians became involved through a GRU (Soviet military intelligence) officer and 'Lucy' began passing information to the Russians through this contact.

Many myths have grown up about the 'Lucy' spy ring. It has been claimed variously that it was a British undercover operation or a Soviet spy ring and the identity of its leader has also been disputed.

The reality is more complex. Its leader was Rudolf Rössler, a Bavarian anti-Nazi who left Germany when Hitler became chancellor, taking refuge in Switzerland. He began publishing anti-Nazi literature and also wrote many anti-Nazi publications, using the pseudonym of R. A. Hermes. Rössler continued to produce literature warning of the evils of Nazism throughout the 1930s.

The outbreak of war in 1939 led to a change in his circumstances. Switzerland was neutral but like other neutral countries it contained elements of both pro- and anti-Nazi sentiment. Brigadier Roger de Masson, head of Swiss military intelligence, then approached Rössler and recruited him as a data analyst for Swiss intelligence.

Rössler was neither a Communist nor working for British intelligence. He was simply an anti-Nazi German who operated a spy ring that passed information to the Soviets and his Swiss employer, Masson.

The name 'Lucy' was given to Rössler's spy ring by his GRU contact Alexander Rado. Rado chose that as its code name because all he knew about the network was that it was based in Lucerne.

Supplying information to the Soviets

There were ten members of the German section of the 'Lucy' spy ring. Seven of the network's members are known and most were high-ranking German officers. Major General Hans Oster was chief of staff and deputy to Admiral Canaris, head of military intelligence in Germany. Another was Lieutenant General Fritz Thiele, deputy head of communications for the German High Command. Other German 'Lucy' informants were General Erich Fellgiebel, head of communications for the High Command; Colonel Rudolf von Gersdorff, chief of intelligence for Army Group Centre; and Colonel Fritz Boetzel, chief of intelligence evaluation for Army Group South East. Two civilian members have been identified as Carl Goerdeler, leader of the 'conservative' opposition to the Nazis in Germany and Hans-Bernd Gisevius, the German vice-consul in

Zurich. The identities of the three other German members remains unknown.

Six 'Lucy' operatives were based in Switzerland: Rössler – given the code name 'Lucy' by Rado; Rado himself, head of the GRU in Switzerland; Xaver Schneider, working for Swiss intelligence; Christian Schneider, working on behalf of Rado and Rössler's intermediary with the GRU; Rachel Dübendorfer, Schneider's boss; and Allan Foote, radio operator and possible MI6 agent.

'Lucy' began in a systematic way when Rössler was approached by Thiele and Gersdorff. They gave him a radio and an 'Enigma' machine, the device used by the Germans to encode their messages. The two men then passed on secret military information to him in the hope that he could find a way to reveal it to the Allies.

The information received by Rössler included invasion timetables, troop movements, casualty figures, equipment losses and production figures. Over the course of five years the Soviets alone received 5,500 messages from him.

His first major intelligence coup was warning the Russians in May 1941 about the impending invasion. He passed on details of the complete order of battle, the times and direction of individual attacks and even German code names.

Rössler first asked Swiss intelligence to pass the information on to the Soviets, but they refused so via his indirect contacts he alerted Rado, who forwarded on the details. They were not believed and Rössler was suspected of being a double agent.

Only after Operation Barbarossa began and the total accuracy of the details he had provided was demonstrated, did the Russians change their minds. From that moment on, any information coming from 'Lucy' was given the highest priority.

Rössler passed on crucial military information, mainly to the Soviet Union, over the next two years. In autumn 1942, he gave them details of the German attacks on Stalingrad and the Caucasus and, in summer 1943, he revealed the detailed German plans for an attack on the Kursk salient, the last German offensive against Russia. The information from 'Lucy' was invaluable to the Soviets in countering the German plans and inflicting a heavy defeat on the invaders at the Battle of Kursk.

Who was behind 'Lucy'?

By the winter of 1942, German intelligence became aware that the 'Lucy' network was sending information on to the Russians. They did not know the source and at first they tried to infiltrate the spy ring with their own agents, but when this failed, they put pressure on the Swiss to close it down. In October 1943, the network's radio transmissions were stopped and some of the agents were arrested by the Swiss.

With his other outlets shut down, Rössler was forced to send his information via Swiss intelligence channels. Fortunately, Masson and others made sure that this data was forwarded to both the Soviets and the Western Allies.

On 9 May 1944, Rössler was arrested by the Swiss authorities and charged with espionage on behalf of a foreign power. He remained in prison at Lausanne until his eventual release on 9 September 1944. The failure of the July bomb plot against Hitler led to the end of the 'Lucy' spy ring. Some of its members died, others were in prison and the remainder had fallen silent.

It has been suggested that the 'Lucy' spy ring was simply a British network using an indirect way of transmitting information to the Soviets but this is highly unlikely. To begin with, the Russians received their information very rapidly, knowing the facts before British intelligence was aware of them. The information was also far more detailed than that which the British possessed. A further objection is the fact that Britain was already passing information directly to Russia from June 1941 onwards. However, Stalin's refusal to share intelligence meant that by the summer of 1942 British intelligence told the Russians almost nothing.

It has also been claimed that Rössler did not exist or had at least adopted a fictitious identity. That is completely untrue. There are detailed accounts of his life before, during and after the war. He was (understandably) a figure of mystery and the 'Lucy' spy ring he headed was one of the most stunningly successful exercises in espionage. Perhaps the last word on the subject should be given to the historian of espionage Ronald Seth. He said: 'Rössler must be ranked among the greatest spies of all time.'

WAS ADMIRAL CANARIS A DOUBLE AGENT?

The Bendlerblock in Berlin stands on a street that has been renamed in honour of Claus von Stauffenberg, one of the leaders of the July 1944 bomb plot that narrowly failed to kill Hitler. During the war, it was the headquarters of the German Navy.

A few years ago, the German Resistance Memorial Centre was opened on the site and tells the stories of those Germans who resisted the Nazis. Names of men like Stauffenberg are now well known and they are no longer regarded as traitors – though most Germans considered them to be so for many years after the end of the war.

One name is conspicuous by its absence: Admiral Wilhelm Canaris, the head of German military intelligence. An exceptionally cunning, devious and ruthless man, he appeared completely supportive of Hitler's policies until 1937, but then his views began to change. He saw that the Nazi leader was endangering the security of his country by risking a global war in which Canaris could only see German defeat as the inevitable outcome.

Canaris remains one of the most controversial and enigmatic figures in the Third Reich. He assisted in detailed planning and intelligence gathering to support Hitler's schemes, but at the same time he also used various channels to warn the Allies of Hitler's intentions. From his position as chief of military intelligence, he shielded many members of the Resistance in Germany, even employing many Jews as agents on his payroll. He also turned a blind eye to the activities of some of his agents when they smuggled Jews out of Germany to safety.

Canaris was not liked in spite of his intelligence. He was considered ambitious, ruthless and self-centred. It is even alleged that he organized (under the Weimar Republic) the deliberate assassination of a potential rival. He never joined the Nazi Party but had many friends who were members. Reinhard Heydrich was a particularly close friend.

On his appointment as head of military intelligence in 1933, he set out to develop a spy network in Spain. He was greatly helped in this by a personal friendship with Franco and his ability to speak fluent Spanish.

Canaris had many Jewish friends and tried to save as many of them as he could. As the Nazis' anti-Semitism grew increasingly virulent, so Canaris became more violently anti-Nazi. As early as 1938 he came to the conclusion that unless Hitler was deposed or assassinated Germany would be ruined. He warned Hitler not to invade Czechoslovakia but to no avail. The admiral was well informed on the Czech situation as he had his own spy network in the country. Ironically, one of its leading members was Oskar Schindler, a Sudeten German who became known to millions of people through Steven Spielberg's film *Schindler's List*. After the Nazi conquest of the country, Schindler was able to use his connections with Canaris to set up his network and draw up a list of Jews from the concentration camps at Auschwitz, Plaszow and Gross-Rosen, using this to save thousands of lives.

The Czech takeover removed any lingering doubts Canaris may have had about Hitler. From now on, he actively recruited as many anti-Nazi officers as possible into military intelligence. One of the most important was General Hans Oster. Oster was one of the first German officers to come to the conclusion that Hitler needed to be assassinated. He soon became Canaris's deputy at military intelligence.

Given Oster's part in the 'Lucy' spy ring, it is possible to speculate that Canaris himself may have authorized him to pass on information. That will never be known with certainty, but the admiral unquestionably tried to sabotage military preparations as much as possible and was definitely in regular touch with anti-Nazi plotters. He also refused to allow any member of the Nazi Party to work for his military intelligence network.

At the beginning of the war, Hitler had high hopes that Spain would allow German troops to pass through it to capture Gibraltar, but Canaris used his personal friendship with Franco to travel to Spain and persuade him to resist the Nazi demands. If Gibraltar had fallen, the result would have been catastrophic for Britain. The Mediterranean would have been dominated by the Axis powers and Britain would have been unable to defend Malta or Egypt. Rommel and his troops could have been supplied easily and the whole Middle East would have fallen under German control or at least its domination.

Franco had his own agenda and the effect of three years of civil war in Spain may have predisposed him to be cautious. Even so, there is no question that any lingering doubts he may have felt – and Gibraltar was certainly a prize worth winning in Spanish eyes – were silenced by Canaris's powerful advocacy of continuing

Spanish neutrality. This was one of the most important actions taken by Canaris to subvert Nazi plans.

Leaks plans to the Allies

Canaris spent the next few years of the war informing the Western Allies of secret German plans. He revealed details of Nazi atrocities in Poland and elsewhere and saw to it that the plans for the German invasion of France, Holland and Belgium were leaked to the Allies.

Not surprisingly, MI6 became interested. Sir Stuart Menzies, head of the department, noted that German military intelligence appeared to be passing on information to the enemies of the country. Was the information trustworthy? Or was it deliberate disinformation? Canaris's reputation for deviousness hindered his credibility in the eyes of MI6. There was also the more general feeling that the idea of the military intelligence network in Germany being run by anti-Nazis seemed completely implausible.

Menzies, either to allay his suspicions or for other reasons that remain obscure, met Canaris on a number of occasions during the war in the neutral countries of Portugal and Spain, but what they discussed has never been revealed. One intriguing possibility is that Canaris may have been involved in undercover joint operations with MI6. British explosives and detonators were used during the July 1944 bomb plot, for example. Canaris had been insisting since 1938 that it was essential to assassinate Hitler, so did Menzies and the admiral discuss ways and means of killing the German leader?

In spite of his friendship with Canaris, Heydrich began to suspect that the admiral was not as fully committed to the Nazi cause as he should have been in his position. However, when Heydrich was transferred to Prague in 1942, he was assassinated by Czech Resistance fighters in league with British intelligence. Could Canaris have somehow been involved in the assassination plot? Heydrich's death certainly took the pressure off the admiral and he was able to continue his activities without disturbance for two further years.

Arrest and execution

The failure of the July 1944 bomb plot saw the growing suspicions about Canaris harden into certainty. However, he and Oster were not arrested until the end of the year, when they were taken to the Gestapo building on Prinz-Albrecht-Strasse and brutally tortured. In February 1945, Canaris and some of his associates were transferred from Gestapo custody to Flossenbürg concentration camp and on 9 April 1945 they were taken out of their cells and hanged.

Canaris left a farewell message to a fellow-prisoner who survived, the former director of Danish military intelligence. The message read: 'I have done nothing against Germany. If you survive, please tell my wife.'

This epitaph for Canaris seems entirely appropriate. He hated Nazism and Hitler with a passion and thought it his patriotic duty as a German to destroy its leader. To him, patriotism was not blind obedience to an evil ruler but an attempt to save his country by overthrowing its nefarious leader and the regime he had imposed upon it.

To call Canaris a double agent is as simplistic and misleading as to call him a traitor. He was a man facing a moral dilemma and he believed that only through the destruction of Hitler and the Nazis could he save the country he loved. In the course of his sustained and effective opposition to the Nazis, he had to carry out actions which under normal circumstances he would never have considered. Canaris felt that he was serving a higher morality by turning against the leadership of his nation and from the vantage point of history it seems impossible to disagree with his assessment

The man who hated Nazism? Admiral Canaris was an extremely hard man to read; he was chief of German counter-espionage, but was he a spy himself?

of the situation. Hitler was in his eyes an aberration and a man who had plunged Germany and the world into a dark abyss. Only by his death and the toppling of his corrupt regime could Germany regain its moral standing among the nations.

WHO WAS 'TOKYO ROSE?'

American troops during the Pacific War were often subjected to Japanese propaganda on the radio from English-speaking female broadcasters. Their programmes were transmitted from Manila and Shanghai as well as Tokyo, but by 1943 all of these English-speaking Japanese women had collectively gained the nickname of 'Tokyo Rose'. The effect of their radio broadcasts on American troops was negligible, however, with almost all of the soldiers immediately recognizing such talk as propaganda.

There has been considerable confusion and perhaps deliberate mystification over the identity of 'Tokyo Rose'. It has been claimed that the 'real Tokyo Rose' was never captured and brought to justice after the war. 'Tokyo Rose' has also been presented as some kind of smouldering seductress and compared to Mata Hari.

In reality, Tokyo Rose was not a single individual but Iva Toguri d'Aquino is the only woman formally tried and convicted of being 'Tokyo Rose'. She was American-born and the daughter of Japanese immigrants to the US. Toguri was visiting a sick relative in Japan when war broke out. As a result, she could no longer stay with her Japanese relatives because she came under immediate suspicion as an American citizen. Nor could she return to the United States because her parents had been arrested and placed in an internment camp. That left her with no means of support and no friends in Japan, so when Radio Tokyo attempted to recruit her as an English-language broadcaster she had little choice but to accept the invitation.

She presented a show called *The Zero Hour* which featured slanted news reports, comedy and American music. One of the soldiers who listened to the programme was interviewed some years later and commented: 'Lots of us thought she was on our side all along.'

At the end of the war, she was briefly detained by American military intelligence but was soon released. Toguri then tried to return to the US but a media frenzy ensued. The FBI was forced to investigate her wartime broadcasts and she was arrested and put on trial.

Facing eight counts of treason – an offence that carried the death penalty – Toguri was acquitted of seven of the charges against her. She was, however, found guilty of one count of treason and sentenced to imprisonment. It was 1956 before she was finally released from prison. In 1974, President Gerald Ford pardoned her after journalists revealed that key witnesses at her trial had been pressured into giving false testimony by the FBI.

Toguri was 'identified' as Tokyo Rose by the media during her trial, but she always rejected that label. The real mystery of the name Tokyo Rose is why it became associated with a single individual rather than being recognized as a composite 'identity'.

WHO WAS THE SPY OF SCAPA FLOW?

One of the earliest engagements between Germany and Britain in World War II was a naval encounter. On the night of 13–14 October 1939, a lone German submarine penetrated the British naval base at Scapa Flow on the Orkney Islands. The U-boat then sailed unchallenged through the defences and sank the *Royal Oak* battleship.

How had this disaster happened? Was it simple negligence or had a German spy provided the U-boat with crucial information about the state of the defences?

Following the sinking of the *Royal Oak*, the Germans held a press conference at which the U-boat captain was paraded. He declared that he had easily evaded the protective booms erected to block the bay. The American journalist William Shirer was present at the press briefing and commented: 'British negligence must have been something terrific.'

That was the verdict by almost everyone at the time. It was also partly justified. The defences at Scapa Flow had been neglected and much of the steel netting had rusted and was no longer effective as a barrier. Churchill raised the issue in September 1939 after his appointment as First Lord of the Admiralty, but nothing was done.

Admiral Sir William French also warned that a submarine could penetrate the defences of Scapa Flow but his message was ignored. The Admiralty remained dismissive about the chances of a submarine breaking through what they considered an impenetrable barrier. They also doubted that the Germans were aware of the poor state of the defences at Scapa Flow. The fact that there was an open channel which, though tight, could be navigated by a submarine was also dismissed.

Sinking of the *Royal Oak*

Unfortunately for the sailors stationed at the base, the Germans not only knew about its weaknesses but also knew about the navigable channel. On 1 October 1939 Commodore (later Admiral) Karl Dönitz summoned a young U-boat captain to meet him on board a ship in Kiel harbour. Captain Gunther Prien was 30 years old and, in the words of Shirer, he was 'a fanatical Nazi'. Dönitz knew that Prien was a daring and skilful U-boat captain, and so he gave him the file on Scapa Flow to read.

Prien studied it carefully during the course of the evening. As he said later: 'I worked through the whole thing like a mathematical problem.' Next morning he reported to Dönitz and agreed to undertake the mission.

On the night of 13–14 October, Prien set sail and safely avoided the blockships that had been sunk in the Kirk Sound channel to prevent access to Scapa Flow, emerging inside the base soon afterwards. At first he headed west but saw no signs of British vessels, then altering his course to the north-east Prien saw two ships lying at anchor. One was the *Royal Oak*.

Prien launched seven torpedoes at the battleship, of which five failed due to steering and magnetic detonator problems, but two torpedoes found their target and the ship exploded and began sinking. The *Royal Oak* carried a crew of 1,146 and 833 were killed in the action. With some difficulty, as he was sailing against a strong current, Prien managed to return home. It had taken less

Adolf Hitler greets Prien after the success of his action at Scapa Flow.

than 15 minutes for him to sink a British battleship in a supposedly impregnable naval base.

Who was to blame?

Scapegoats were immediately demanded for the disaster. French had warned of the poor state of Scapa Flow's defences and yet he was blamed for these failings and dismissed. The head of MI5 was also blamed for failing to identify what, in the Admiralty's view, must have been the result of a German spy network on the Orkney Islands. MI5 agents were immediately sent to investigate, but failed to find any evidence of Nazi spies.

In 1942, the American magazine the *Saturday Evening Post* ran an article by the émigré Curt Reiss. This claimed that Dönitz had been informed of the poor state of the Scapa Flow defences by Captain Alfred Wehring, who was said to be a former World War I German naval officer who had settled in Switzerland after the German defeat. He then began working for German intelligence, according to Reiss, using the 'cover' of a watchmaker and jeweller. In 1927 he moved to Britain, using the fictitious name of Albert Oertel and four years later he moved to the Orkney Islands. He then opened a jewellery shop on the islands, but his real role was to spy on Scapa Flow for the Germans. The information he sent back to Germany purportedly allowed Dönitz to plan the raid. Reiss added that Wehring boarded Prien's *U-47* submarine before its entry to Scapa Flow and acted as a pilot, guiding it through the narrow channel.

Walter Schellenberg, one of Himmler's closest associates, confirmed the story in his autobiography. He wrote:

> *The sinking of the battleship took less than 15 minutes, but 15 years of patient and arduous work by Alfred Wehring had*

been the necessary foundation for this supremely successful mission.

The dismissed head of MI5 also declared that: 'The Germans had been supplied with up-to-date information by a spy.'

On the face of it, this is conclusive evidence but the truth is more complex. It is telling that Dönitz, the man who authorized Prien's operation, made no mention of any spy in his autobiography.

Post-war journalists also investigated Reiss's claims and found that his story lacked hard evidence. He gave no sources for his account and interviews with islanders produced no evidence that anyone resembling Wehring/Oertel had ever lived on Orkney. One resident told the journalists: 'I am convinced beyond possibility of doubt that such a person has never existed and is only a journalist's fabrication.'

Even more damaging for the story is that German naval archives contain no records of either a Captain Alfred Wehring or an Albert Oertel.

So what is the truth about 'the spy of Scapa Flow'? Why did Schellenberg repeat Reiss's story in his memoirs? Why was MI5 so convinced that German spies must have discovered the weaknesses of Scapa Flow and used the information to launch Prien's daring raid?

Naval complacency was certainly a factor, though it was unfair to make French the scapegoat for the poor state of Scapa Flow's defences when his warnings on the matter had been dismissed by the Admiralty. Reiss's phantom 'fifth columnist' Wehring/Oertel is either an exercise in creative journalism or deliberate disinformation by German intelligence. Schellenberg was one of the best exponents of disinformation that the Germans possessed and his memoirs, published posthumously in any event, may have simply reflected a wish to brag about the efficiency of his spy network. Equally, British intelligence may have preferred to blame a German spy rather than admit to their own complacency and incompetence.

In spite of these caveats there *was* a real German spy who provided the navy with information about Scapa Flow. Captain Horst Karle was sent by naval intelligence to the Orkneys in August 1939, returning with a detailed survey of the defences at Scapa Flow as well as reporting gossip he had heard from locals. This information was passed on to naval intelligence and was the basis on which Dönitz formulated his plan of attack. If anyone deserves the title of 'the spy of Scapa Flow', Karle is the only credible candidate.

THE D-DAY LANDINGS DECEPTION

There is no doubt that the Allies were far more sophisticated and successful than the Germans in terms of the disinformation they supplied to the enemy. The 'Man Who Never Was' made the invasion of Sicily easier than it might have been and also contributed to the German defeat at the Battle of Kursk.

In spite of having been comprehensively fooled by the Allies in 1943, the Germans were also deceived about the D-Day landings in 1944. Even Hitler realized that the Allies would invade northern France, but he believed that his Atlantic Wall could hold them.

Operation Overlord, the Allied plan for the invasion of France, took a year to prepare. Along with the complex and detailed military and engineering work, an extensive campaign of disinformation was launched to mislead the Germans.

The deception plotting was given to two leading MI5 officers, Thomas Robertson and John Masterman. They had already enjoyed striking success in countering German espionage and by 1942 every known German spy in Britain had been 'turned' into a double agent.

The deception planners knew that the invasion would come somewhere between Cherbourg and Dunkirk. Calais was the most obvious invasion point. It was the closest to Britain and the shortest distance for ships to travel and it also had two large deep-water ports. Capturing it would also open the road to Paris and the German industrial heartland of the Ruhr.

Hitler certainly expected the Allies to invade via Calais. He told his generals that: 'It is here that the enemy must and will attack, and it is here – unless all the indications are misleading – that the decisive battle against the landing forces will be fought.'

Not only was Calais the 'expected' target but it was also heavily defended. As early as July 1943, Allied military planners had concluded that it was too dangerous to land there and that northern Normandy was a more promising target.

The original date for the invasion was set for 1 May 1944, but stormy weather in the English Channel forced its postponement until 6 June.

Robertson and Masterman were not involved with the military planning of the operation. Their role was to mislead the Germans into believing that the attack would come via Calais and therefore tie down German forces in the wrong area. They also set out to deceive the Germans about the strength, objectives and timing of the invasion.

Double agents feed false data

Using a number of double agents whom, amazingly, German military intelligence trusted implicitly, Robertson and Masterman fed the Germans with false data. These spies were among the most bizarre and amateurish exponents of espionage ever recruited which may explain why they were so successful.

Two of them were women. Elvira de la Fuente Chaudoir was a bisexual Peruvian who fed false information to Helmut Bleil, a German spy who reported directly to Goering. Another female agent on the team was Lucy Sergiyev, a Parisian of Russian descent. She was totally obsessed with her dog and when it was killed by a car she became convinced that British intelligence were responsible. Sergiyev's seething anger did not lead her to turn on her employers, but she was perhaps the least enthusiastic of all the MI6 spies.

The Polish pilot Roman Czerniawski sent numerous false radio messages to Germany. These were read and believed by German military intelligence and his 'information' was regarded as completely reliable.

Juan Pujol García was a Catalan fantasist who began by approaching the British to work as a spy but was rejected by them. He then went to the Germans and offered his services. They accepted him, but García made no attempt to provide them with any genuine information. Instead, he simply told the Germans what he believed they wanted to hear.

His 'information' was so amateurish and so often wrong that when MI5 discovered who he was it commented that it was 'a miracle that he has survived so long'. He was quickly recruited and used to send thousands of letters in invisible ink and over a thousand false radio messages. The Germans swallowed this cascade of disinformation without question.

Perhaps the most successful of all these double agents was the Serbian Dusko Popov. For five years he posed as a Yugoslav businessman and travelled between Britain and Portugal. By August 1941, the Germans had become so pleased with his false reports that they sent him to America. Although that mission ended in disaster, with both the FBI and the Germans being suspicious of him, by October 1942 he had managed to completely convince the Germans of his sincerity. He was soon being described by them as 'the best man the Abwehr [German military intelligence] has'.

In 1944 Popov provided the Germans with a detailed but entirely fictitious account of Allied plans. His military intelligence controller was so impressed that he confidently told Berlin that 'the landing in western Europe will not take place until next spring'.

Germans fooled

German intelligence, relying entirely on the false information they were fed by these double agents, became convinced that attacks on Norway and Denmark by British forces were imminent and that Calais was certainly the invasion point for France.

These deceptions were also fed by the phantom manoeuvres of a fictitious US Army group led by Patton. An equally non-existent British 4th Army was said to be preparing for the invasion of Denmark and Norway. Dummy tanks and similar devices fooled German aerial reconnaissance into expecting the assault to fall anywhere except Normandy.

What is surprising is that the Germans, having already fallen victim to the deception of Operation Mincemeat in 1943, were so comprehensively fooled about the D-Day landings. They had no spies on the ground in Britain except for the double agents who were working for the British and there is no doubt that they overestimated the strength of the Atlantic Wall. Calais was certainly a logical place for the Allies to attack, but the Germans should have at least considered alternatives.

Even after the landings on the beaches of Normandy the Germans, misled by the false data they had received from the British spies, continued to regard it as a diversionary raid and still expected the main attack to come via Calais. It took them seven weeks to realize the truth and by that time the Allies were well entrenched and winning the war in northern France.

CHAPTER ELEVEN
MISSING OR DEAD?

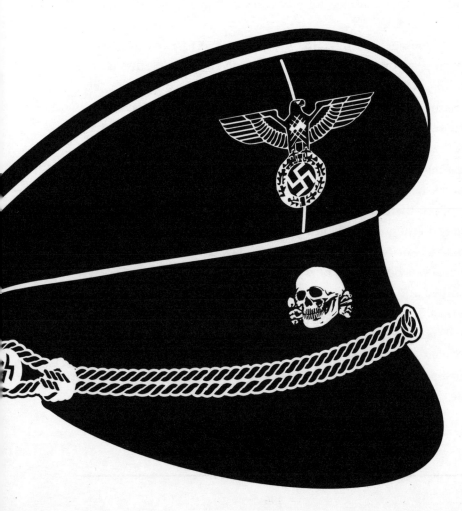

THE FATE OF HERSCHEL GRYNSZPAN

Herschel Grynszpan was 17 years old when he assassinated Ernst vom Rath, a foreign service officer in the Paris embassy. There is disagreement over the reasons for his actions and whether or not he survived the war.

Grynszpan was born in Hanover, but Hitler's appointment as chancellor turned him into a refugee. At the age of 14, he applied for a visa to Palestine but was turned down. The reasons for his rejection are in dispute, with some claiming that it was because of his youth and others citing his physical weakness. He then tried to find work as a plumber but rampant German anti-Semitism made that impossible.

At the age of 15, he attempted to move to Paris. He held a Polish passport as well as a German one and hearing that border guards in both France and Germany were refusing to let Jews pass he decided to enter France illegally. First he travelled to Brussels and stayed there for a few days and then he took a tram that ran between Quievran and Valenciennes. Having heard that passengers without baggage were rarely subjected to security checks, he boarded the tram and arrived safely in France.

Once there he made his way to Paris. To his dismay, France was adopting a hostile attitude towards Jewish refugees and he spent a year trying to legitimize his stay. On 11 August 1938, his appeal was denied and he was given four days to leave France. He escaped and continued to live in hiding. The French police failed to track him down, but he lived in fear of imminent deportation.

When his passports expired and he had nowhere to go, the terrified and disillusioned youth frantically sought a way out. Most people who have studied the subject believe that an event in late October 1938 drove him to assassinate vom Rath.

Herschel Grynszpan, the German-Polish casual worker of Jewish descent, who shot Ernst vom Rath in front of the German embassy in Paris, 1938.

Grynszpan's parents, brother and sister were taken from their home in Hanover by the Nazis and sent to the Polish border town of Zbasyn. Then on 16 October the Polish government, itself viciously anti-Semitic, issued a decree aimed at the Jews, which announced that all Polish citizens living in Germany would have their passports cancelled and be denied the right to re-enter Poland. Not wishing to have thousands of Polish Jews left in Germany, the Nazis frantically deported all Jews who held Polish citizenship.

When these unwilling deportees arrived at the border, they were met with equal intransigence by the Poles. The Polish authorities refused to admit them, so the Jews were marooned between the two border stations. Grynszpan's family were among the stranded Jews and it was when his sister told him of their plight that he decided to act.

Shooting and arrest

Grynszpan shot vom Rath twice in the abdomen at the German embassy in Paris on 7 November 1938. He died two days later and the Nazi reaction was immediate and appalling. On the night of 9–10 November, the Nazis launched *Kristallnacht*, the worst pogrom seen in Germany for hundreds of years. Thirty thousand Jews were sent to concentration camps, Jewish shops and businesses were looted and destroyed and synagogues were burned down. These were not the actions of random thugs but brutality organized and directed by the SS.

Grynszpan's assassination of vom Rath became headline news, particularly in Germany. Goebbels seized on it as 'proof' of 'the Jewish conspiracy' and it dominated the German media.

Many other countries carried the news. The American journalist Quentin Reynolds compared Grynszpan to Gavrilo Princip, the man whose assassination of Franz Ferdinand had begun the train of events leading to World War I. A week after the killing, the CBS journalist Dorothy Thompson ran the story on the radio. An appeal fund was launched on Grynszpan's behalf in the United States which raised $30,000 in a month and Thompson used this money to hire a top European lawyer to defend him. Then public interest faded as more pressing international problems came to the fore.

Grynszpan was remanded in custody at Fresnes Juvenile Prison in Paris and remained there until the German capture of the city in June 1940. The French authorities then sent him and other prisoners to the south of France, but the train carrying them was attacked by German aircraft and in the confusion he managed to escape.

Bizarrely, he applied for admission to two French prisons. One was at Toulouse and the other at Bourges. Toulouse refused to admit him, but Bourges received him as an inmate and, on 18 July 1940, he was transferred to Germany. From that point onwards, his fate is conjectural.

Not long after the war ended, one of Grynszpan's defence team claimed that he had been beheaded by the Germans soon after his transfer from Bourges to Germany in 1940. There is no evidence for this claim and it is directly contradicted by Nazi records.

When Grynszpan passed into their custody the Nazis planned to make him the star 'witness' in a spectacular 'trial' which would 'prove' to the world that a vast Jewish conspiracy existed and was entirely responsible for the war. There were prosecution witnesses ready to testify and a large dossier of 'evidence' had been compiled.

Even Grynszpan's line of defence was recorded. He claimed that he and vom Rath were homosexual lovers and that his action in killing him was not politically motivated but a crime of passion. This claim was almost certainly a lie, but it helped to muddy the waters and delay his trial.

In 1952 Michael Soltikow published two articles on Grynszpan. They claimed that the young man was a homosexual and that the murder was indeed sexually rather than politically motivated. Then in 1957 historian Helmut Heiber wrote a paper on Grynszpan claiming that he was still alive and resident in Paris under a false name. Heiber's assertion was picked up by the editor of a New York newspaper and re-asserted as the truth. Later the New York journalist changed his mind and simply stated that his death remained a mystery.

Did Grynszpan survive?

November 1959 saw a further article asserting that Grynszpan was alive. Its author, Egon Larsen, added that he went back to Paris at the end of the war and changed his name. He then obtained work in a garage and was later married with two children.

In December 1959, the Paris magazine *l'Arche* ran an article confirming Larsen's claims. This led to the hiring of Andreas Freund from Associated Press to research the matter further. Freund discovered that there were no German documents reporting Grynszpan's death, that a relative of vom Rath believed that Grynszpan was still alive, that the West German government had refused to pay reparations to Grynszpan's father for the death of his son and that a French police officer was still in touch with Grynszpan.

Grynszpan's father had indeed requested a reparations payment for the death of his son in 1958, but Heiber gave the court in Hanover his reasons for believing that Herschel was still alive. He stated that there were reports of Grynszpan being in Brandenburg Prison in 1945. Walther Hammer, archivist in Hamburg, had told Heiber that Grynszpan was transferred on 20 January from Hamburg to Magdeburg and another source had told Heiber that Grynszpan was in Hamburg.

Interpol also became involved and stated: 'The information that Grynszpan might be living in Hamburg under a false name is based on unsubstantiated reports transmitted by an employee of the French security police in Baden-Baden in 1954. This information has never been confirmed.'

However, the court in Hanover concluded that Grynszpan was probably dead and eventually Heiber abandoned the idea of his survival.

Perhaps the most thorough investigation into the matter was undertaken by the French doctor Alain Cuenot. He accepted that Grynszpan was still alive in 1942 but believed that he died soon afterwards. Cuenot also obtained information from Fritz Dahms, a former foreign affairs ministry employee and one of the leading Nazi officials involved in Grynszpan's trial. Dahms told Cuenot:

> *The death of Grynszpan occurred shortly before the end of the war, but I am no longer able to say if he died of natural causes or if he lost his life by violence. At the time, the Foreign Affairs Ministry received no precise details on the manner in which he died.*

Cuenot points out that there is extensive documentation from 1942 for the planned trial but nothing subsequent to that date.

> *If Grynszpan had survived the years 1943, 1944 and 1945, it would seem quite unusual that documents would not have been added to those already gathered.*

There is also the fact that Grynszpan was treated extremely well during his confinement. He received ample food and his conditions were comfortable. There is no doubt that the plan to use him as a star witness in a show trial – and Hitler's personal interest in the Grynszpan case – make it unlikely that he was murdered. Cuenot concludes that the young man probably died of an illness and that accounts for the sudden absence of further records. It may even be, he suggests, that because Grynszpan died in spite of his exceptionally favourable treatment his custodians may well have tried to conceal his death even from the authorities. That could at least partly account for the sudden air of mystery.

Cuenot is probably correct in these assertions. Certainly the young man survived for two years in Nazi captivity, but it is unlikely that he lived beyond that. The truth about his fate may never be known and the mystery of his survival continues to be disputed.

MARTIN BORMANN

By the time the Third Reich collapsed in flames and bloodshed one man had made himself the second most powerful person in Germany. Martin Bormann rose steadily up the ranks of the Nazi Party and after Hess's flight to Britain he became close to the centre of power.

By 1945, he was one of a tiny handful of 'true believers' who remained completely loyal to Hitler. Trapped in Berlin, a city on fire from aerial bombardment and encircled by Russian troops, his resolve never wavered. When Hitler and then Goebbels committed suicide in the bunker, Bormann decided not to follow their example. Instead he planned to escape from the doomed city and make his way to Schleswig-Holstein where Admiral Karl Dönitz presided over what remained of the Third Reich.

His first attempt at saving himself was to send General Krebs under a flag of truce with an offer to surrender the Reich Chancellery if its occupants were guaranteed safe passage. The

Russian general Chuikov insisted on unconditional surrender, however, and refused to give any guarantees to the residents in the Chancellery.

A thwarted Bormann then decided to break through the Soviet lines and try to link up with Dönitz. At 4.30 p.m. on 1 May 1945, he put his plan to the inmates of the bunker. Most dismissed it as unworkable, but a few decided to take the risk.

At 8 p.m. that evening, a small group, including Bormann, left the Reich Chancellery, climbing unsteadily over the piles of rubble and past the scenes of death and devastation. Making cautious progress, the party arrived at the Weidendammer Bridge. They planned to cross the River Spree and head north-west towards Schleswig-Holstein.

Martin Bormann (right) walks alongside his master Hitler and Joachim von Ribbentrop at the Wolf's Lair in East Prussia. Leading Nazis had to go through Bormann to get to Hitler, a process he deliberately made frustrating.

CHAPTER ELEVEN

There is considerable debate over what happened next. Two of the survivors gave entirely different accounts of events to the Nuremberg War Crimes Tribunal. Erich Kempka, Hitler's chauffeur, declared:

> *Several tanks came along, followed by some armoured personnel carriers. The tanks broke through the road block on the bridge. Bormann was just behind the leading tank, which became a target. It was hit by an anti-tank rocket fired from a window and blew up. Where Martin Bormann had been there was now just a ball of flame.*

Kempka's account is contradicted by the testimony of another member of the party, the senior Hitler Youth leader Artur Axmann, who stated that:

> *The ammunition-laden Tiger Tank exploded. I instinctively took refuge in a bomb crater. So did several others. Bormann was there, together with Hitler's surgeon Dr Stumpfegger, State Secretary Naumann, Schwägermann [Goebbels' adjutant] and my own adjutant, Weltzin. They were all uninjured. We sat in the bomb crater and tried to work out the best way of getting out of Berlin.*

According to Axmann, the group made its way to the Lehrter train station, but they found it occupied by Soviet troops. Managing to evade them, they made their way to the Moabit district. Axmann's account continues:

> *On the return journey through the Invalidenstrasse we came under heavy fire. Shortly after we crossed the tracks at the*

Lehrter station we saw two men lying on the ground. They were Martin Bormann and Dr Stumpfegger. A mistake was out of the question; we could clearly see their faces.

Both Kempka and Axmann declared that Bormann was dead, even though each gave a different account of his demise. Kempka has testified to many events and in general has proved to be a trustworthy witness, but the testimony of Axmann, a much more senior Nazi, has at times been shown to be unreliable. His only corroborating witness was Weltzin, who died in a Soviet prison camp. On the whole, if Bormann did die on that day, Kempka's account seems the more plausible version of his last moments.

Other witnesses declared that they saw the two bodies mentioned by Axmann. Both were buried on 8 May. One body was identified as Stumpfegger's through documents found on his clothes but the witnesses were unable to identify the second man's corpse.

For many years, there has been speculation that Bormann survived. Generally these theories place him in South America. Brazil, Argentina and Paraguay are the most common locations for his post-war residence.

Like the various accounts of Bormann's death, the theories of his survival contradict one another. Jakob Glas, his chauffeur, claimed to have seen him alive in Germany in late 1945, while former British Army captain Ian Bell, a war crimes investigator, maintained that he saw Bormann boarding a ship in Bari, Italy. When he alerted his superiors, he was told to follow it but was warned: 'Do not apprehend.'

Reinhard Gehlen, former Nazi and head of post-war intelligence for West Germany, claimed that Bormann escaped to Paraguay, but historian Ladislas Farago said that he fled to Argentina and was actively assisted by the Perón regime. A totally different story comes from Christopher Creighton, a former British naval intelligence officer, who said that Ian Fleming was part of 'OPJB', a clandestine operation to spirit Bormann out of Berlin in 1945.

Simon Wiesenthal, the tireless Nazi hunter, also believed until 1972 that Bormann escaped. He declared as late as 1966 that Bormann was 'alive and living on the Chile–Argentine border using the name Ricardo Bauer'.

Possible US involvement

Operation Paperclip was a project at the end of the war to recruit former Nazi and Japanese scientists into the service of America and Britain. Those singled out for such favour were often given new identities before they worked for their new employers. The Russians also recruited former Nazis into their sphere of influence.

The suggestion is that Bormann, being too notorious simply to recruit openly, as had occurred with men like von Braun, was smuggled out to safety and given a new identity. A false account of his death was then released to the world. This appears superficially plausible, but there are serious problems with the theory.

In the first place, Bormann had more blood on his hands than most Nazis, so it is almost inconceivable that he would knowingly have been ferried to safety without protests. Even Stalin, who suggested that Hitler might have survived the war, made no such claim about Bormann.

In any case, it is arguable whether Bormann had much to offer the Allies in return for sparing him. Unlike Dornberger, von Braun and other Nazis recruited through Operation Paperclip, he was not a scientist and had little in the way of skills to offer. Essentially, Bormann was a glorified filing clerk who had enjoyed too much power under the shambolic leadership of Hitler.

This objection is met by two counter-claims, neither of which has ever been substantiated. One is that Bormann controlled the Nazi finances and had access to the looted treasure, gold reserves and other assets. He is said to have offered them to the Americans in return for his safety.

The other counter-claim is even more outlandish. It argues that Bormann surrendered German enriched uranium to the United States on a U-boat, *U-234*. Also, it is claimed, he passed on German atomic secrets and possibly even a functioning nuclear weapon.

Two facts are mentioned in support of this theory. One is that a list of German and Austrian scientists was compiled by the commander of the Gestapo's scientific section, Werner Osenberg. US Navy captain Ransom Davis used Osenberg's list as the basis for recruiting scientists under Operation Paperclip.

Osenberg was captured in 1945 and interned in Germany, but he was soon transferred to France. There he liaised with the Allies in providing the names of scientists whose recruitment would be useful.

Bormann's involvement is suggested on the basis that he would have known about and had access to Osenberg's files. Bormann was also close to Gehlen, post-war chief of West German intelligence, and SS Colonel Otto Skorzeny.

It has been suggested that General Patton's military campaigns against Nazi secret projects were so precise and accurate that his information could only have come from an 'inside' source, who could well have been Bormann.

A second argument in favour of this idea is the fact that the German physicist Rudolf Fleischmann was flown to America to be interrogated not long before the USA dropped the atomic bomb on Hiroshima. Why was his expertise required so urgently? Were there some last-minute problems with the Manhattan Project?

It is highly probable that Osenberg's list assisted Operation Paperclip in recruiting German scientists and Bormann would almost certainly have known the contents of the list. But that is irrelevant to the question of Bormann's survival. The same is true of Fleischmann's sudden trip to America. His expertise bears no relationship to the issue of Bormann's whereabouts. Interesting though these facts are, they have no relevance to Bormann's fate.

South American link

In 1972, a skull was discovered in Berlin and declared to be Bormann's. It was discovered at a building site, only a few metres from where retired postman Albert Krumnow – at the time still a serving soldier – claimed to have buried him. The skull was matched with dental records and was confirmed to be that of Bormann.

There were glass splinters in the jawbone of the skull and traces of prussic acid, suggesting that he had bitten down on the glass ampoule containing the poison. In other words, he had committed suicide, like Hitler, Eva Braun, Goebbels, Himmler and Goering. Perhaps Kempka and Axmann knew that he had killed himself and preferred to say that he had died a more heroic death.

A West German court formally declared Bormann dead in 1973 and for many people, including Wiesenthal, that ended the idea of Bormann's survival. Then in 1998 mitochondrial DNA testing was performed on the skull, which confirmed that it belonged to Bormann. The test results were published in 2003.

Others felt that the skull raised as many questions as it answered. Where were the other remains of Bormann's body? Why had it taken so long for it to be found? And why had only a mitochondrial DNA test been carried out rather than full DNA profiling?

There were also two strikingly anomalous features about the skull. One was that it revealed traces of dental work using techniques that were not developed until the 1950s. The second anomaly is that the skull was encased in a type of red clay that is not native to Germany but common in parts of Paraguay.

These results are troubling. They seem to suggest that the skull is Bormann's and the clear evidence of suicide by prussic acid supports the idea of his death in 1945. However, the anomalies suggest that he may have survived and spent at least some time in Paraguay, possibly dying there. Perhaps he died in 1972 and steps were then taken to relocate his skull to Germany.

The accounts of his death are conflicting and contradictory but so are the accounts of his survival. There is no doubt that some Nazis escaped to South America, where several countries had long-established communities of German descent.

South American politics were volatile. Paraguay under President Stroessner – his very name betrays his German ancestry – was a brutal military dictatorship. Its government was markedly sympathetic to the Nazis, however, and it made no attempt to turn over war criminals to other countries, so Bormann would have been safe and welcome in such a sanctuary.

In 1964, Reinhard Gehlen passed a document to the Paraguay interior ministry. It claimed that Bormann died of cancer in Asunción in 1959, after being tended by Dr Josef Mengele. On his death he was buried in Ita in an unmarked grave.

David Irving has also pointed out that the contents of Bormann's coat were stolen by Soviet soldiers and later reappeared in Russia. The corpse next to Bormann's was certainly his fellow-escapee Stumpfegger.

The balance of probability remains in favour of Bormann's death in May 1945, but there are enough doubtful factors to make it possible that he may have been the one major Nazi who eluded death or capture. We will probably never be certain of his fate.

ADOLF HITLER

There are numerous claims for Hitler's survival, in spite of the fact that witnesses saw his dead body and destroyed it. Most theories about his escape place him in South America, though one exercise in fantasy journalism 'reported' him as 'assisting Saddam Hussein' during the First Gulf War!

There are three main arguments in favour of the survival of Hitler. One is the response of Stalin, who initially declared that the remains found in Berlin were those of Hitler and Eva Braun and then later announced that they were not. There is little doubt, though, that Stalin had an entirely political motive for creating a mystery around the issue of Hitler's death and the consensus among all serious researchers into the subject is that Hitler did commit suicide in 1945.

Two other principal sources support the 'survival' story. The first is a set of recently released FBI files claiming that Hitler faked his death and escaped to safety in South America.

One of these files was a letter from an 'informant' to a reporter on the *Los Angeles Examiner*, which contained the third-hand 'information' that 'Hitler and his party' had 'landed from two submarines in Argentina approximately two and one-half weeks after the fall of Berlin'. When the reporter tried to follow up the story, he was unable to do so. Even his 'informant' had vanished from sight. Nor did a check by police and immigration (the source claimed to be an Argentine exile) reveal any trace of his existence. All this story shows, however, is that the FBI followed up a lead and found nothing.

The time given for the alleged submarine landings of Hitler – two and a half weeks after the fall of the Reich – rules out *U-530* and *U-977* – the only two Nazi submarines that did not surrender at the end of the war, but eventually surfaced in Argentina some months later. It is clear that the story is a sensationalist piece of fiction with no supporting evidence in its favour.

Another claim is that a photograph shows Hitler in Brazil with his girlfriend – given the suspicious name of 'Cutinga' – and using the alias of Adolf Leipziger. The photo is of poor quality and it is almost impossible to distinguish the faces of the individuals adequately. It is no accident that the photo was 'discovered' at the same time that the woman who 'found' it was trying to get her book on Hitler published, but it has no credibility as evidence.

Every recorded 'sighting' of Hitler catalogued by the FBI turned out to be a dead end, even though it is clear that the FBI took these claims seriously and investigated them thoroughly. No evidence of Hitler's survival was ever discovered.

The CIA also became involved in the quest for Hitler and a recently declassified CIA memo reports that a former German soldier told a CIA agent in Venezuela that he had 'met an individual who strongly resembled and claimed to be Adolf Hitler'. Another CIA memo states that the same 'informer' claimed that Hitler was using the name Adolf Schrittelmayor. He also told the agency that Hitler had 'left for Argentina' in January 1955.

The CIA's response is telling. They wrote that neither the agent who had been contacted nor the agency 'is in a position to give an intelligent evaluation of the information, and it is being forwarded as of possible interest'. So the 'evidence' is no more than the unsupported word of someone who had told a CIA agent that he had met Hitler. This information has never been corroborated either by the agency or any other source.

There is also the fundamental problem of Hitler's basic nature. It is possible to imagine men like Bormann leading a life of obscurity in exile but a man like Hitler would have found it impossible to keep quiet or control himself. In any event, he was in such poor health by the end of the war that the idea that he could have survived into the 1980s or 1990s – as some of the more exotic survival claims suggest – is impossible.

In Bormann's case, there is some reason for doubt, even though the balance of probability is that he died in May 1945. Hitler, though, is a different matter and the question of his survival may help to fuel conspiracy theories, but it has no credibility. The founder and destroyer of the Third Reich almost certainly died by his own hand in the bunker in Berlin.

HANS KAMMLER

There is some doubt over the question of Bormann's survival, but there is no reasonable doubt that Hitler perished in the bunker at the end of April 1945. With SS General Hans Kammler, however, it is quite possible that he may have survived the war.

As with Bormann, the accounts of Kammler's supposed death in May 1945 are inconsistent and contradictory and his body has never been found. Kammler was a civil engineer whose primary responsibilities were building projects. He was a strong German nationalist and, on 1 March 1932, he joined the Nazi Party. Once Hitler became chancellor, he began to organize Nazi building projects.

In May 1933, Kammler joined the SS, where he soon found favour with Himmler. He was rapidly promoted within the organization and, by June 1941, he was given responsibility to construct, develop and enlarge concentration camps. This included fitting them with gas chambers and crematoria. He also oversaw the construction of underground facilities for V-2 rockets and Me 262 jet planes at Mauthausen and the unfinished underground network in the mountains of Silesia.

He made extensive use of slave labour, particularly after 1941, and four million 'workers' came under his control. Once the workers were too ill to continue, Kammler simply executed them. He was listed by the Allies as one of the most wanted Nazi war criminals.

The trail becomes mysterious from April 1945 onwards. On 4 April 1945, British troops captured an underground bunker near Lübeck where they found abandoned staff cars and, according to some sources, Kammler's body.

But whoever the body belonged to, it cannot have been Kammler's as he met Speer on 13 April and continued to issue orders until the end of the month.

Another story has it that Kammler died in May 1945 at a bunker in Prague that had been captured by Czech partisans. One version claims that Kammler either ordered his adjutant to shoot him or he killed himself while an alternative account places him in Prague, but has him escaping on 9 May with a group of other Nazis. The rest of them, so the story goes, surrendered to American forces at Pisek in southern Czechoslovakia, but Kammler preferred to commit suicide, either using cyanide or by shooting himself.

This last version is supported by the testimony of Kammler's driver, Kurt Preuk, who gave a sworn affidavit to a Berlin court on behalf of Kammler's wife. She had petitioned the court to declare her husband dead. Preuk claimed that he had driven Kammler out of Prague and, on 9 May, had been ordered to leave the road and drive into a forest, where Kammler shot himself. Preuk and others buried his body and continued their journey. The Berlin court accepted Preuk's statement and, on 7 September 1948, officially declared Kammler dead.

This sounds conclusive, but Preuk later contradicted his sworn statement. In 1959, he claimed that Kammler had died 'on or around 10 May 1945' and that he was uncertain of the cause of his death.

Then in 1965 Heinz Zeuner, an SS man who was also one of Kammler's drivers, claimed that his death was as a result of taking cyanide and that it had occurred on 7 May 1945. Further confusion resulted when German researchers discovered more information about Kammler and his drivers in government archives.

This additional information involves Zeuner and another of Kammler's drivers, SS man Friedrich Baum. Zeuner claims that, when the Czech partisans rose up in Prague on 6 May 1945, they attacked Baum's car, wounding him in the left knee. The two of them managed to drive to safety, but Baum had to go to hospital in Prague. A few days later partisans captured the hospital and killed him.

Other records refer to the death of Sergeant Friedrich Baum from the Berlin Motor Pool. He was apparently admitted to hospital at Gmunden in Austria on 23 May 1945 and the records state that he was wounded in the knee at Prague on 4 May 1945. His leg then became infected and had to be amputated. He died in hospital on 29 May and was buried in a military cemetery.

There are two problems with this version of events. One is that German Army records have no Sergeant Friedrich Baum listed. That is probably easy to explain because, like many SS members, he might have pretended to be an ordinary German soldier. A more serious difficulty is the nature of his wound. Both Zeuner and other witnesses testify to the attack on the car in Prague and all claim that it was Baum's left knee that was injured. However, the hospital records state clearly that it was his right knee which was injured and his right leg that was amputated.

Was he recruited by the US?

Whatever the truth about Baum, Kammler certainly vanished from sight. What is more surprising – leading to suggestions that he was spirited away by the Allies as part of Operation Paperclip – is that he seems to have disappeared from the Allied 'radar'. At one stage, he was listed as the third most 'wanted' name on the list of war criminals and yet his name hardly appeared in the Nuremberg Trials documentation.

Kammler appears to be an unlikely candidate for Operation Paperclip. He was not a scientist and could have offered little to the Allies in return for his safety. Instead, he was a bureaucrat who controlled vast construction projects. Perhaps, in spite of the brutality of his slave labour empire, he seemed unimportant in comparison with other leading Nazis. Or perhaps he knew far more than has been assumed.

The idea that Kammler was spirited away by the Allies has received strong support from the testimony of John Richardson – son of Donald Richardson, a personal adviser to Eisenhower – and recently declassified American archives. His possible survival was examined in a television documentary and the historians Rainer Karlsch and Mathias Uhl believe it is probably a true account of what happened to Kammler.

These sources claim that the Americans took Kammler prisoner and that the CIC (Counter Intelligence Corps) interrogated him. Donald Richardson was in charge of his debriefing. In the documentary, John Richardson revealed that his father had been tasked with spiriting Kammler out of Germany and giving him a new identity. As he told the programme:

This engineer brought a special treasure from the Third Reich into the United States. He offered modern weapons for us.

The programme suggested that the various stories of Kammler's death were deliberately faked by the Allies and varying versions of his suicide were designed to muddy the waters still further. His knowledge of German secret weapons programmes made him a prized catch in the eyes of the Americans.

The accounts of Kammler's death are certainly inconsistent and vague and Zeuner and Preuk both contradicted themselves when they told their stories. It is possible that the Baum who died in Gmunden hospital may have been Kammler disguising himself as an ordinary soldier and using his driver's name to conceal his true identity.

Kammler may well have shot himself, taken poison, been shot by his adjutant, died in a hospital of his wounds or somehow made his escape to safety. All of these scenarios are possible, but in the light of the new revelations the Operation Paperclip theory is perhaps the most plausible. If he escaped, he was capable of fading into anonymity as Eichmann and Mengele did and, if he died, the circumstances are unclear and the location of his grave is unknown. The true fate of slavemaster Kammler will probably always remain a mystery.

HEINRICH MÜLLER

Heinrich Müller was the feared chief of the Gestapo, a career policeman who was recruited to the Gestapo by Heydrich and became one of its most senior and ruthless members. He was a participant in the notorious Wannsee Conference in 1942 where the Final Solution – the extermination of the Jews – was presented to the Nazi leadership. Until 1942, he reported directly to Heydrich and then, following his assassination, to Himmler.

Müller is described by Professor Johannes Tuchel as a 'bureaucrat'. Like Eichmann, he simply carried out orders. In the course of his 'career' under the Nazis, he 'was responsible for mass crimes, deeply involved in the Holocaust, attended the Wannsee

Conference and was responsible for the mass killings of Soviet prisoners of war'.

He was certainly sought after by the Allies, but the last sighting of him was in the Berlin bunker two days after Hitler's suicide. From that point onwards, he vanished. Many people have speculated that he escaped as no trace of his body was found and there were no known accounts of his death.

However, Tuchel's researches into Müller uncovered a crucial piece of evidence. At the end of the war, a gravedigger buried a man in uniform in the Berlin-Mitte Jewish Cemetery. When Tuchel compared the documents and decorations found on the body with German archives and files from the CIA they matched Müller's details.

The Jewish Cemetery in Berlin contains the grave of the famous German Enlightenment thinker Moses Mendelssohn, which was vandalized by the Nazis. Many victims of Allied bombing raids were buried there in mass graves and nowadays the cemetery is a Jewish memorial and a place of pilgrimage. It is ironic, therefore, that the final resting place of one of the architects of the Holocaust appears to be within a Jewish cemetery.

In the absence of a DNA examination, the fate of Müller will never be known with certainty. However, Tuchel has shown from documents that his most probable end was during the last stages of the war and that he probably lies in a mass grave in the Jewish Cemetery in Berlin. The Jewish religion forbids exhuming bodies, so he will perhaps remain there.

RAOUL WALLENBERG

Raoul Wallenberg was a Swedish diplomat and businessman. During the war he saved the lives of thousands of Hungarian Jews.

From 1938 onwards, under the dictatorship of Admiral Miklós Horthy, Hungary had passed numerous laws placing restrictions on Jewish participation in government, imposing a strict quota on the numbers who could enter certain professions and even forbidding marriage between Jews and non-Jews. These measures created difficulties for Wallenberg's business partner in Hungary, Kálmán Lauer, so Wallenberg found himself forced to act on Lauer's behalf and travelled to the country extensively. He soon became fluent in Hungarian and was able to make contacts among the people.

Passport photo of Raoul Wallenberg, Swedish architect, businessman and diplomat, who saved thousands of Jews from the Holocaust. The picture was taken in June 1944.

For all Horthy's anti-Semitic policies, he had not introduced the horrors of the Final Solution to his country and after the German defeat at Stalingrad he began secret peace talks with Britain and America. This enraged Hitler, who occupied the country and put Horthy under house arrest. A more pliable puppet was then installed, but the real power now rested with the German military governor, Edmund Veesenmayer, an SS officer.

In April 1944, Veesenmayer began to deport the Hungarian Jews to the extermination camps in Poland. Eichmann was the main organizer of these forced deportations and he 'achieved' a total of 12,000 Jews a day.

Wallenberg was then asked to represent the War Refugee Board in Hungary. Under pressure from the Americans, the Swedish government assigned him to their embassy in Budapest and in July 1944 he arrived at his new post.

Protective passports

By that time, Eichmann had already deported 400,000 Hungarian Jews, most of whom were sent to Auschwitz and murdered. However, there were 230,000 Jews still left in Hungary and Wallenberg set out to do what he could to save them. He issued 'protective passports' which identified those possessing them as being Swedish citizens (and thus not subject to deportation orders) and Hungarian and German officials were bribed to allow others to escape.

Next, Wallenberg rented 32 buildings in Budapest and declared that they were part of the Swedish embassy and therefore under diplomatic protection. Signs such as 'The Swedish Research Institute' or 'The Swedish Library' were affixed to their doors and Swedish flags were hung at the front of the buildings. These soon became a sanctuary for 10,000 Jews.

Wallenberg even climbed on to the roof of a train full of Jews about to be deported to Auschwitz and began handing out protective passes to the passengers, in spite of demands by the Germans that he should climb down. Then the Hungarians began shooting at him, but he continued to hand out the passes. Both the Germans and the Hungarians were stunned by his actions. They admired his courage and allowed him to carry on until he had no more passes left. He then ordered all the passengers in possession of the documents to leave the train and walk to a nearby group of waiting cars.

On 29 October 1944, Soviet troops under Marshal Rodion Malinovski attacked Budapest and by the end of December the city was completely encircled. Wallenberg was then summoned by Malinovski to his headquarters in Debrecen on 17 January 1945 to defend himself against charges of espionage. He told his friends that: 'I'm going to Malinovski's … whether as a guest or prisoner I do not know yet.'

He was then arrested by the Russians and from that point onwards his fate is uncertain. On 8 March 1945 Hungarian radio – by then firmly under the control of the Soviets – announced that Wallenberg had been murdered on his way to Debrecen. It was implied that he had been killed by the Gestapo or the Hungarian fascist group the Arrow Cross. The Soviet account of his death was accepted by the Swedish government and that appeared to be the end of the matter.

Did Wallenberg survive?

Unfortunately, there are several other accounts of Wallenberg's death, all inconsistent, as well as various accounts testifying to his survival. On 6 February 1957, the Russians released a document dated 17 July 1947 which declared that 'the prisoner Wallenberg died suddenly in his cell this night, probably as a result of a heart attack or heart failure.' The document was signed by the head of the Lubianka prison hospital.

Another Russian declaration was made in 1991, this time following an investigation by the government into Wallenberg's fate. The conclusion of this inquiry was that he had been executed in Lubianka prison in 1947, possibly poisoned.

A further claim came in 2000 when Alexander Yakovlev said that he had been told by Vladimir Kriuchkov, former head of the Soviet secret police, that Wallenberg had been shot. He did not explain why he had been killed.

Another claim was that Wallenberg had been poisoned by the NKVD (forerunner of the KGB/FSB). August 2016 saw the discovery of a diary by KGB chief Ivan Serov in which he wrote: 'I have no doubts that Wallenberg was liquidated in 1947.'

On the other hand, various claims for his survival have been made. In February 1949 a German prisoner of war claimed to have seen Wallenberg in a transit camp in Kirov. Not only did he see him but he heard him tell the German officer that he was a Swedish diplomat and was in Soviet custody 'through a great error'. Then Greville Wynne, a British spy imprisoned by the Russians, testified that he had talked to a man in Lubianka prison who claimed to be a Swedish diplomat.

Another claim, this time by a Russian, is that he was seen on Wrangel Island in 1962. A woman prisoner also claimed to have seen Wallenberg in the 1960s in a Russian gulag. Various other 'sightings' of Wallenberg continued until the late 1980s, with the locations given as various prisons or psychiatric hospitals.

The general consensus and the strong probability is that Wallenberg was murdered at some point in 1947. What was baffling for many years was why the Russians arrested him.

There is no doubt that he was a great humanitarian who saved thousands of lives. What was not generally known, however, was that he was also working for the OSS (the predecessor of the CIA). Various documents released by the CIA confirm that he was 'an agent of OSS' and that he was acting as a link man between them and the Hungarian Resistance fighters. This at least provides some rational basis for the Soviets' treatment of him. Their own spies and agents in Hungary would almost certainly have been aware of Wallenberg's activities and it has been suggested that it was Vilmos Böhm, a Hungarian politician and Soviet agent, who betrayed him to the Russians.

It is difficult to come to a final conclusion since much of the material on Wallenberg remains classified. This is particularly true of the Russian archives. The most likely explanation is that Wallenberg's links with the OSS and the Hungarian Resistance made the Soviets suspicious and that once they had arrested him he was probably held in prison for a year or two before he became of no further use and was murdered. There remains the possibility that he may have survived much longer but the truth will almost certainly never be known.

CHAPTER TWELVE

NAZIS IN ANTARCTICA

The Hungarian emigrant Ladislao Szabó was the first person to claim that there were secret Nazi bases in Antarctica. His claim was made as early as July 1945 and involved an escape by Hitler to the Antarctic in a German U-boat. Later, the Holocaust denier Ernst Zündel sketched out these claims in more detail. Others, particularly Howard Buechner, elaborated even further on these stories.

Buechner was primarily interested in 'sacred relics' such as the Spear of Destiny, which was alleged to have pierced Christ's side as he hung on the Cross. He was apparently contacted by someone claiming to have been part of a mission to smuggle the spear to safety in an Antarctic base. Buechner said he was called Captain Wilhelm Bernhart, but admitted that this was not his real name. 'Bernhart' claimed that he had taken the spear by submarine to Antarctica in 1945 and also helped 'a group of German businessmen' to recover it in 1979 during the 'Hartmann Expedition'. Buechner was shown a letter allegedly signed by Hartmann, along with some photographs and the log of the expedition. According to Bernhart, Captain Maximilian Hartmann – another pseudonym – had been entrusted with the task of conveying the spear to Antarctica along with other treasures of the Reich. In 1979, the 'Hartmann Expedition' had recovered it and taken it back to Europe and it was now in the possession of an esoteric order calling itself the Knights of the Holy Lance.

BYRD'S EXPEDITION

The Germans certainly claimed Queen Maud Land for Germany and renamed it Neu Schwabenland (New Swabia). An expedition in 1938–39 explored the region and took a number of photographs of it. That much is admitted by everyone, but precisely what the expedition discovered and whether or not any kind of German 'colony' was established there has been fiercely disputed.

Buechner claims that the expedition found several ice-free regions and discovered lakes and vegetation in the interior. This leads on to the story of Station 211 (sometimes called Point 211), a supposed German base in the land. Buechner does not mention it in his books but other writers certainly do. Believers in Station 211 make much of the words of Admiral Karl Dönitz in 1943, when he is alleged to have declared:

> The German submarine fleet is proud of having built for the Führer, in another part of the world, a Shangri-La on land, an impregnable fortress.

Station 211 is generally located within an ice-free mountain in the Mühlig-Hofmann mountains of Neu Schwabenland. It is claimed by Buechner and other writers that the Antarctic expedition of 1946–47 led by Admiral Byrd was really a military invasion of the continent aimed at destroying the Nazi stronghold at the South Pole. Their claim is that Byrd was defeated by the superior Nazi technology and forced to retreat.

Buechner does not mention Station 211 but suggests an alternative location in the same region. He claims the crew placed their cargo at the foot of a glacier in the Mühlig-Hofmann mountains, digging it deep into the ice and protecting it with steel plates. This story is clearly fantasy. It would have involved the crew discovering one of the few areas not covered with shelf ice before venturing deep into the interior carrying over a ton of steel. Apart from the logistical difficulties, some regions of Antarctica have up to 60 ft (18 m) of snow in a year. After even twenty-five years, this cargo would have been buried so deeply that it would have been impossible to retrieve it. Nor does it make sense to trek to an ice-free region and then bury the cargo in the ice. If it really existed, Station 211 would be a far more plausible place to conceal Nazi treasures.

Byrd's expedition to the South Pole was a disaster, with injuries and fatalities and little in the way of positive results. All of the deaths and injuries seem to have been the result of accidents, although the George One aircraft crash is attributed by conspiracy theorists to the result of anti-aircraft fire from Nazis anxious to keep the Americans at bay. The idea that the Nazis in Antarctica were able to repel a full-scale American invasion is of course pure fantasy.

Between 1956 and 1960, a Norwegian expedition set out to map Queen Maud Land on the basis of aerial photographs and land surveys. They did discover an ice-free mountain that was a perfect match for the description of Station 211 and called it Svarthamaren (the black hammer). This region was designated as a 'specially protected area and site of special scientific interest' in 1978. It was described as being an 'exceptional natural research laboratory for research on the Antarctic petrel (*Thalassoica antarctica*), snow petrel (*Pagodroma nivea*) and south polar skua (*Catharacta maccormicki*), and their adaptation to breeding in the inland/interior of Antarctica'.

ARGENTINE CONNECTION

Naturally, conspiracy theorists see this designation of the area as a ploy to prevent the Nazi stronghold from being discovered. They may be correct in suspecting that there are reasons besides natural history for keeping this area of the Antarctic private, but the idea that the motivation for such actions would be to conceal a secret Nazi base is fantasy.

Argentina also plays a part in the alleged Antarctic base. It is known that some Nazis were able to escape to South America and find refuge in Argentina, Brazil, Chile and Paraguay. There is no doubt that German submarines continued to be active in some way with the collusion of the Peronists then in power in Argentina.

The mysterious surrenders to Argentina of two German U-boats on 10 July 1945 and 17 August have been examined already. Advocates of a Nazi base in Antarctica seize on their voyages as 'proof' of their claims.

More evidence of a Nazi–Argentine connection was provided by the Agence France-Presse, which stated on 25 September 1946: 'The continuous rumours about German U-boat activity in the region of Tierra del Fuego between the southernmost tip of Latin America and the continent of Antarctica are based on true happenings.'

NAZI TREASURES

Many years later the 'Hartmann Expedition' went to Antarctica to recover the 'Holy Lance' and other treasures of the Third Reich. In 1969, Rudolf Hess went into hospital to have an ulcer treated. A few days later a former crew member of *U-530*, one of the submarines that surrendered to Argentina after the end of the war, was given the key to a box in a Swiss bank. This box then led to another one which contained a number of sealed envelopes. The message was signed 'H'.

When the crewman opened the envelopes, they gave him instructions to deliver the contents of the box to the man who was the custodian of the Spear of Destiny and other Nazi treasures. In Buechner's book, he is named as Colonel Maximilian Hartmann.

Hartmann remained in Germany after the war, but some of his last actions were to ensure that Martin Bormann and other senior

Nazis were spirited out of the country by submarine. The crew-man gave the envelopes to Hartmann and their contents excited him. One was a message from Karl Haushofer revealing the exact location of the bronze boxes sent to Antarctica at the end of the war.

The second envelope instructed Hartmann to recreate Himmler's Knights' Grand Council under a new name, the Knights of the Holy Lance. This order was supposedly dedicated to the goal of establishing world peace. The third envelope contained money with which Hartmann was required to institute the Knights of the Holy Lance and recover the Spear of Destiny from its hiding place in Antarctica.

Buechner declared:

> The group now had a vastly different purpose. The major objective of their new direction was the attainment of world peace. They also put the reunification of their homeland as a central goal. Of overriding importance was the need for the power and guidance of the Holy Lance.

After a series of adventures that read like something out of a pulp fiction plot, Hartmann and three other Knights arrived in Antarctica by helicopter. They were able to locate and remove the steel plates guarding the entrance to the Holy Lance's hiding place in Antarctica. On discovering the entrance, they saw a steel-lined tunnel leading further into the mountain which extended for ten metres. Inside the tunnel, they saw frozen pillars of ice and came to a smaller cave within the tunnel. The cave contained a room which held 'the Reich treasures'. A small obelisk marked the spot and on the obelisk was an inscription reading: 'There are truly more things in heaven and "in" earth than man has dreamt (beyond this point is Agharta) Haushofer 1943.'

According to the 'log' of the expedition, they saw eight large bronze chests. The eight men were disappointed to find that they could only carry four of them back to the helicopter.

When they opened the chest containing the spear they saw 'a faded leather case' inside which was 'the Holy Lance'.

Buechner claims that Hartmann and his fellow explorers returned to Brazil where they were able to obtain false papers for the spear, presenting it as an art object. They passed through customs unchallenged and most of the expedition members returned to Germany. Hartmann then went on to America, where he met a former U-boat sailor. Buechner claims this sailor was given a log of the expedition by Hartmann and a signed letter testifying to its authenticity. He then returned to Germany with the spear. Buechner claims that the spear is now in the possession of the Knights of the Holy Lance.

Himmler enters the picture at this point. It is claimed that he imagined that by sending a Nazi colony to Antarctica he would be able to preserve the Aryan race in a secure environment. He used submarines to transport weapons, tools, raw materials, equipment and people to the base in the South Pole.

ANTARCTIC REICH

Much of this additional layer of Nazi Antarctic lore is added by Konstantin Ivanenko. He claims that as early as 1942 Himmler had created a new 'military unit' of blond-haired and blue-eyed women between the ages of 17 and 24. All were tall and slim and wore sky-blue uniforms. These young women were members of the *AntarktischeSiedlungensfrauen* (Antarctic Settlement Women or ASF).

According to Ivanenko, 10,000 Ukrainian women, half of them 'ethnic Germans' and the other half Ukrainians who had been declared 'racially pure', were transported from Ukraine to the Antarctic, along with 2,500 German men. These were mainly soldiers, though a few were engineers and scientists. The soldiers who went to Antarctica with these 'racially pure' women were the legendary 'Last Battalion'.

This outpost in Antarctica is said to have survived a full-scale invasion by the US under Byrd and Ivanenko declares that:

> *The total population of Nazis in Antarctica now exceeds two million and many of them have undergone plastic surgery in order to move about with greater ease through South America and conduct all manner of business transactions.*

He adds that what he calls 'the Antarctic Reich' is 'one of the most militarily powerful states in the world' which is able to 'destroy the USA several times over with its submarine-based nuclear missiles'. Ivanenko claims that Neu Berlin, the capital, is located in 'narrow sub-glacial tunnels' under a mountain and is heated by 'volcanic vents'. In a supreme touch of fantasy, he claims that Neu Berlin is next to 'the prehistoric ruins of Kadath, which may have been built by settlers from the lost continent of Atlantis well over 100,000 years ago'. Kadath, of course, was an entirely fictitious land created out of the vivid imagination of the American writer of horror stories H. P. Lovecraft.

Barabou Veda (almost certainly another pseudonym) adds his own details about the Nazi base in Neu Schwabenland. He claims to have spent the first 15 years of his life on the base where, surprisingly, the language spoken by the inhabitants was not German but English or 'Indian'.

Veda claims that aliens live on the base and work closely with the Nazis. At one point he suggests (without a trace of irony) that empty Coca-Cola cans represent a 'trade' between the Nazis and the aliens for the extraterrestrials' superior technology. Perhaps it is no accident that he was diagnosed with schizophrenia on his emergence in Germany and spent time in a mental hospital.

The Antarctic region of Neu Schwabenland was, according to Vladimir Terziski, extensively colonized by submarines and ships carrying people and material to their underground base in the South Pole. The people included 'several hundred thousand concentration camp slave labourers' along with scientists and Hitler Youth members who dedicated themselves to recreating the Third Reich at their polar base. He claims that there is 'a vast underground city' with 'a population of two million' and a capital city called New Berlin. Their principal activities are genetic engineering and space travel.

Branton (yet another pseudonym) is if anything even wilder in his claims than Terziski. He claims that the SS continue to live underground and conduct genetic experiments. There was, according to Branton, a 'German-Nazi-Illuminati pact' between them and 'the serpent races'. Branton believes that he has been abducted by aliens since his early childhood and that many of his abductions involved CIA underground bases. He claims to have met 'hybrids', Nordics, Telosians, 'orange' aliens and Sasquatch.

Branton maintains that as well as the Nazis landing on the Moon and Mars, the Marconi Company also landed on Mars in 1956. He believes that from their Antarctic underground bases the Nazis were able to continue developing their advanced weapons until they achieved the capability of flying into space and establishing colonies on the Moon and Mars and that they possess 'interplanetary dreadnoughts'.

Some of the stories recounted in this chapter might well be flights of fancy, but it cannot be denied that huge scientific achievements in terms of advanced technology, aviation, weaponry and even space research were accomplished under the Nazis. It is small wonder that the existence or otherwise of secret Nazi bases in Antarctica continues to give rise to a host of conspiracy theories.

CHAPTER THIRTEEN
MISCELLANEOUS MYSTERIES

THE NAZI GHOST TRAIN

The Nazi 'ghost train' is often confused with the Nazi 'gold train'. The gold train may or may not have existed, but so far no evidence for it has been discovered.

By contrast, the Nazi 'ghost train' was real. It was a train that carried political prisoners and Allied pilots held at the Saint-Gilles prison in Brussels to German camps. On 2 September 1944, the train was filled with 41 Allied airmen and 1,370 political prisoners.

Its failure to transport the POWs and political prisoners to Germany was due to Belgian railway workers. They knew that Allied troops were on the outskirts of Brussels, so they deliberately delayed the train's departure for long enough to force the Germans to abandon the idea. Instead, the Germans released the political prisoners at Klein-Eland/La Petite-Ile station in Brussels and used the train to return troops to Germany to defend their homeland.

The train was formed of 30 goods wagons and was loaded up with its original group of passengers at Brussels Midi railway station, ready for an early morning departure. However, deliberate obstruction by Belgian railway workers prevented it from leaving until almost 5 p.m. Additional delays meant that it could only reach Mechelen/Malines by the evening and even then it had to be diverted to Muizen to take on more water. On the following morning, acts of sabotage further delayed the train as it left Muizen station and it was forced to return to Klein-Eland/La Petite-Ile station at 10.15 a.m. The train's journey was then halted by the removal of the locomotive and the pretence that no suitable replacement could be found.

The Red Cross then began to negotiate with the Germans and they agreed to release the political prisoners. Once they had been removed, German troops boarded the train, but it only progressed as far as Schaerbeek before it was deliberately sent into the shunting yards. Several wagons became derailed and had to be abandoned and the Allied airmen, who had not been released, took advantage of the chaos to escape. The Germans eventually managed to get the train started once more and headed off to Germany.

The 'ghost train' was not really a 'ghost', though, because the Belgian railwaymen and even the Germans knew where the train was throughout the proceedings.

THE BRITISH PRISONERS IN AUSCHWITZ

A Polish historian working for the Auschwitz Museum discovered the names of 17 British prisoners held in Auschwitz. It was a chance find that occurred while he was sifting through debris from a bunker in Monowitz concentration camp, also called Auschwitz III by the Nazis. Labourers at the slave labour camp worked for the IG Farben rubber company. Alongside this camp was a prisoner-of-war camp known as E715, whose inmates included several hundred British prisoners. These prisoners also worked as slave labourers.

Fourteen of the names on the list can still be distinguished, though three are illegible. The names of the inmates that can be deciphered are Osborne, Lawrence, Gardiner, Lamb, Symes, Saunders, Dunne, Dunn, Hutton, Holmes, Clark, Manson, Auty and Steinger.

The names were discovered written in pencil on a card. Six of the names – Gardiner, Dunne, Dunn, Holmes and Clark as well as one name that is still illegible – have check marks against them. This probably indicates that the prisoners are dead.

The identities of most of the prisoners are unknown. 'Gardiner' has been identified as James William Gardiner, who served in the Royal Artillery. He was killed by 'friendly fire' in an American air raid and is buried in the Rakowicki Cemetery in Kraków.

Experts are uncertain as to the status of these inmates. Some claim that they were Jewish prisoners of war sent to die at the camp while others suggest that they might be a British SS division that fought with the Nazis during the war. The most probable explanation is that, particularly given their location in the POW section of the camp, they were British soldiers or airmen who had been captured by the Germans and were being held in perhaps the worst possible POW camp in Germany.

Polish historians have contacted British military archives in the hope of identifying the other 16 soldiers on the list.

It is known that prisoners of war – British and other nationalities – were held at Auschwitz. Many of them were forced to work as slave labourers for IG Farben.

They saw brutality and even murder and at least one of them was shot dead by a guard for refusing to climb a girder in freezing weather. There were several hundred British prisoners alone in Auschwitz, so it is highly probable that the 17 names listed on the German record were among them – men who instead of being treated under the rules of the Geneva Convention were forced into slave labour and witnessed genocide. Few of those who survived wished to talk about their experiences.

RUSSIAN ANTI-TANK DOGS

During the German invasion of the Soviet Union the Russian military used specially trained dogs to carry explosives. They were sent to attack tanks, armoured cars and any other military target. The original plan was for the dogs to leave the bomb and return to their trainers, but repeated trials with this system failed. Instead, the Russians fitted the dogs with bombs that detonated on impact and killed the animals as well as the enemy.

The dogs were not trained by the military but by police, hunters and circus animal trainers. Animal scientists also became involved, to make the programme more effective.

After a number of failed trials, the bomb was attached to the dog and it was trained to locate enemy tanks. When it made contact with its goal, the bomb was detonated. Training included keeping the dogs hungry and placing their food beneath tanks. As the dogs adapted, the training was modified to include 'battle simulations' such as gunfire, running tank engines and similar events.

Dogs were fitted with mines weighing 10–12 kg (22–26 lb), which were carried in two individual canvas pouches. The mines, which carried no markings, were fitted with safety pins that were removed immediately prior to sending the dogs into action. Wooden levers protruded from the pouches and, when the dog went beneath the tank, the lever hit the underside and detonated the explosive charge.

Thirty dogs and 40 trainers were sent to the front line at the end of summer 1941. Problems were immediately identified in terms of the dogs' usefulness for war. They had been trained with static tanks and refused to budge when a tank was moving. Also, gunfire frightened many dogs and they ran away, which sometimes led to the bombs attached to them exploding and killing Russian soldiers. Only four of the original 30 dogs were able to detonate their mines near German tanks and it is unclear how much damage they caused. Six certainly killed Soviet troops on their return and three more were shot by the Germans.

A further mistake was that the dogs were trained on Soviet diesel tanks rather than German petrol tanks. This meant that the dogs were attracted to the familiar smell of the Russian tanks, which again made them dangerous to their own side.

The programme enjoyed some successes in spite of these difficulties. At Hlukhiv, six dogs managed to cripple five German tanks and near Stalingrad 13 German tanks were destroyed by dogs. Equal success was enjoyed at the Battle of Kursk when

12 German tanks that were attacking the Soviet line were put out of action by 16 dogs. Once the Germans became aware of the Soviet anti-tank dogs, they took extreme measures to deal with them. Every German soldier was instructed to kill any dog he saw, even those that were not directly involved in combat.

By 1942, the Russians seem to have lost interest in the project. From then on, they mainly trained dogs to seek out mines and also used them for delivery purposes. In spite of this, a scaled-down programme of training anti-tank dogs continued until 1996.

How effective the dogs were as weapons against tanks is disputed. Soviet authorities claimed that they damaged or destroyed 300 German tanks, but most modern historians – even Russian – regard this as propaganda. They certainly achieved some success, but the fact that the strategy was effectively abandoned in 1942 suggests that its effect was marginal at best.

Between 1941 and 1942, 40,000 dogs were used in a variety of combat roles by the Soviet Army. However, German soldiers considered them to be ineffective and, even if the official Soviet figures are to be believed, the sacrifice in canine lives did not remotely achieve a comparable rate of destruction of German tanks. Forty thousand dogs achieved at best – and even this figure is highly unlikely – 300 successes.

THE 'CURSE OF TIMUR'S TOMB'

The Mongol chief Timur, immortalized by Christopher Marlowe in *Tamburlaine the Great*, was a ruthless warlord who conquered vast swathes of territory. In India, he built a pyramid out of 70,000 human skulls. It is claimed that he killed around 17 million people, although this is probably an exaggerated figure.

When he died, he was laid to rest in a mausoleum that is considered an outstanding example of Mongol architecture. Some of its features were replicated on the later Taj Mahal. His final resting place is in what is now Uzbekistan.

Today only the tomb's foundations, one of the four original minarets and the entrance remain.

There are two inscriptions on the tomb. The first, written on the tombstone, says: 'When I Rise from the Dead, the World Shall Tremble'; and the second, this time inside the tomb, proclaims: 'Whosoever Disturbs My Tomb Will Unleash an Invader More Terrible than I.' This second inscription gave rise to the legend of 'the curse of Timur's tomb'.

Stalin ordered Timur's tomb to be opened in 1941 and two days later Operation Barbarossa began. The Nazis invaded the Soviet Union and initially carried all before them. Three elderly men warned the excavator of the tomb of 'Timur's curse', but no notice was taken. The continued failure of the Russians to hurl back the Germans led Stalin to reconsider. He ordered Timur's body to be returned to his tomb and be given a full Muslim funeral. In December 1942, his corpse went back to its resting place and from that time onwards the tide of war began to turn and the Nazis were gradually defeated.

Did Stalin unleash the 'curse of Timur's tomb'? Did his actions in returning the body of the conqueror to its mausoleum change the course of the war?

Coincidence or not, it is a fascinating sidelight on World War II.

THE MYSTERY OF DUNKIRK

May 1940 saw what appeared to be a decisive moment in the war. German troops moved through Belgium to attack France and French and British troops were sent to the area to repulse them.

Allied commanders, even before the Mechelen Incident, had expected the German invasion of France to be effectively a re-run of the World War I Schlieffen Plan. This avoided the Ardennes and struck at France through south-west Belgium.

However, the German High Command in discussions with Hitler had decided on a risky but in their opinion more worthwhile line of attack.

Tanks were intended to provide the cutting edge of the invasion force. Moving rapidly through the Ardennes they could trap the British Army in Belgium, cut off the French forces and then march towards Paris.

This plan in many ways resembled the route taken by the Prussian Army in 1870, when they defeated the French at Sedan. The Allied commanders should at least have considered the possibility of this approach but it played no part in their thinking. Instead they remained obsessed with the idea that the main German thrust would come through Belgium and that any German manoeuvres in other sectors of the Western Front were purely diversionary.

Disinformation

Admiral Canaris assisted this monomania with a skilful campaign of disinformation. He had already deceived the Allies earlier in 1940 about the invasions of Norway and Denmark, which took the British and French completely by surprise. Now he set out to give the impression that the main German thrust against France would come through Belgium.

The French commander, General Maurice Gamelin, the chief of the Imperial General Staff Sir Edmund Ironside and the chief of the British Expeditionary Force General Lord Gort all swallowed the bait. Gamelin and Ironside were almost ecstatic at the thought that the Germans were about to follow a plan that had failed in World War I. Orders were issued to send the bulk of the French Army into Belgium to launch an attack on German positions.

This was more than the Germans could have hoped for. They had expected Gamelin to divide his forces and keep the Ardennes route defended as well as the Belgian approach. But in spite of the misgivings of General Alphonse Georges, who advised him to adopt that course of action, Gamelin committed most of his forces to the Belgian attack. The French 7th Army further reduced the Allies' defensive capabilities in the Ardennes by advancing towards Breda in Holland. Georges was horrified at what he saw as an unnecessary gamble, but Gamelin overruled him with disastrous consequences.

Their rapid advances encountered little or no opposition. The Luftwaffe was conspicuous by its absence and some British officers became concerned. Kim Philby, combining his career as a spy with that of war correspondent for *The Times*, told an American journalist: 'It went too damn well. With all that air power, why didn't he bother us? What is he up to?'

The Allies soon discovered the answer to that question. German troops were in Holland and Belgium but only in sufficient quantities to deceive the enemy troops. Gamelin, confident that the Ardennes terrain was too difficult for tanks to penetrate, refused even to consider the possibility of a German attack from that quarter.

While the Allies were marching ever northwards, the German tanks moved slowly and completely unnoticed through the Ardennes. On 12 May, they crossed the River Meuse and pressed forward relentlessly. Their advance created a 50-mile (80-km) gap in the Allied line and the limited French defences in the region collapsed as tanks and aircraft pounded them into submission.

Allies decide to retreat

It was three days before the enormity of the situation dawned on Gamelin. Not only were the German troops preparing to advance on Paris, but the British and French forces in Belgium and Holland were now forced to retreat in a desperate attempt to salvage the situation.

The military fiasco was compounded by a failure to collaborate adequately. The British troops had no idea of the seriousness of the French situation and began to grumble that the French troops were not pulling their weight. Gamelin appeared incapable of decisive action and, on 19 May, he was dismissed, being replaced by General Maxime Weygand.

Then Gort complained that he was receiving no clear instructions from Britain. He wrote bitterly that 'the entire lack of higher direction' was 'terribly wearing on the nerves of all of us'. Eventually Churchill ordered him to counter-attack, but by that time it was too late. Gort wrote indignantly: 'How does he think we are to collect eight divisions and attack as he suggests?'

Frustrated at the lack of progress, Churchill sent Ironside over to give Gort orders to attack. He told Ironside that neither the British nor the French forces were capable of carrying out these instructions. Reluctantly Gort agreed to lead a small force from Arras to the south.

Ironside then talked to the senior French commanders on the ground and found them completely demoralized, but after some heated exchanges they agreed to move their forces to the north to link up with the British. When Ironside returned to give him the news, Gort responded that he believed 'they would never attack'. He was quite right; when the British attacked Arras, the French remained inactive.

At this point, Weygand proposed a new angle of attack for the French to follow. The Germans had driven a wedge between the Allied positions and Weygand believed that his plan could avert disaster. By now, however, Gort had lost all hope of recovering the situation and announced that he would begin evacuating the British troops immediately. Faced with a flat refusal by Gort to consider any alternative to retreat, Weygand was forced to abandon his plan. Whether it would have been successful is open to question, but in the event his ideas were never put to the test.

Evacuation plan

Gort's decision to retire forced the British to hastily devise an evacuation plan which was known as Operation Dynamo. On 26 May the first British troops left Dunkirk to sail home. Ironside was in despair at the prospect. He blamed 'the incompetence of the French High Command' and believed that Britain would be lucky to save more than 30,000 of its troops.

The British troops waited on the beaches for the Panzers and the German infantry to advance upon Dunkirk. There is no doubt that if they had done so the port would have fallen and the bulk of the British Army would have been captured.

But the expected ground assault did not come. The German tanks and troops held back and instead the Luftwaffe pounded away at the soldiers. However, a combination of fog, poor visibility and the heroism of the RAF greatly hindered their efforts. British pilots flew nearly 3,000 sorties to protect the troops and by 4 June a total of 337,000 troops, 110,000 of them French, had been successfully evacuated.

The Royal Navy carried the bulk of the armed forces, but hundreds of little boats also came across from Britain to help rescue the troops. It was an astonishing achievement in the face of overwhelming odds. What could have been a disaster turned into almost a triumph.

There is no doubt that the failure of the German tanks and infantry to attack Dunkirk was a decisive mistake. If they had moved against the Allied troops, it is difficult to see how more than a handful could have escaped.

For all the heroism shown at Dunkirk and the successful evacuation of the bulk of the Allied troops, it was a humiliating defeat. Hitler ordered bells to be rung for three days in celebration and Churchill said grimly: 'Wars are not won by evacuations.'

Troops evacuated from Dunkirk arrive back in England, 1940.

Dunkirk did represent a military defeat, but the consequences would have been much worse if the troops had been captured. It is hard to see how Britain could have continued the war effectively with the bulk of its army gone.

Why did Rundstedt stop?

Ever since there have been differing viewpoints on why the Germans relied on the Luftwaffe rather than attacking with tanks and ground troops. Hitler has been accused of ordering them to halt, either out of a wish not to destroy Britain or simple misjudgement; Goering has been accused of overconfidence and of boastfully telling Hitler that the Luftwaffe could finish the job on its own.

What is known is that Field Marshal Gerd von Rundstedt ordered his troops not to attack. Rundstedt knew that half of his tanks were unserviceable and he wanted to keep the remainder for the forthcoming attack on the French forces.

Rundstedt's decision gave the defenders of Dunkirk three days to strengthen their positions and evacuate the troops. Hitler then ordered Rundstedt to attack, but by then the bulk of the forces had already been evacuated. After the war, the German tank commander Heinz Guderian speculated on what would have happened if Rundstedt had taken a different decision. He wrote:

> What the future course of the war would have been if we had succeeded at the time in taking the British Expeditionary Force prisoner at Dunkirk, it is now impossible to say.

Realistically, its capture would have made any kind of military action by Britain impossible. The navy and the air force would have protected the island to the best of their ability but the Germans would have been emboldened to attack Britain directly.

Rundstedt's over-caution at Dunkirk can now be seen in hindsight as one of the greatest blunders of the war, becoming a turning point in the conflict. Dunkirk was a defeat but it could have been a catastrophe. From the vantage point of history, it can be seen as the first stone in the foundations that led to eventual victory.

BLUNDER OR CONSPIRACY?

At the end of World War II, the political situation in Europe was in a state of flux. Britain and America had been allied with the Soviet Union against the Axis powers and there was still considerable public goodwill towards the Russians.

At the Yalta Conference, Stalin, Roosevelt and Churchill agreed on 'spheres of influence' for their respective nations at the end of the war. Under the terms of the meeting, eastern Europe was effectively placed in the Soviet sphere of influence. A fig leaf of democracy was agreed upon, but Churchill and Stalin – the degree of Roosevelt's complicity is still fiercely controversial – knew that in practical terms it meant the annexation of eastern Europe at least. Stalin also had designs on Greece, Finland, Austria and even Italy, but these nations were not specifically 'assigned' to the Soviets.

Even during the final five months of the war in Europe, strategic decisions were taken which made the Soviet conquest of eastern Europe infinitely easier. There is continuing controversy over whether these military choices were a recognition of the reality on the ground, a naïve trust in Soviet good intentions and sincerity, the result of being blinded by Nazi propaganda into imagining that German resources were stronger than they actually were or a conscious act of betrayal.

Montgomery's troops were closer to Berlin than any other Allied forces and the general was anxious to advance upon it

Field Marshal Gerd von Rundstedt shortly after his capture by the 7th United States Army in 1945 – he was seized in a hospital at Bad Tölz where he was undergoing treatment for arthritis.

quickly and capture it ahead of the Soviets. Militarily he could easily have done so as by that stage Berlin was only lightly defended and the German troops were mainly engaged on other fronts of warfare. However, Eisenhower ordered him not to do so but instead to send his troops to the south of Germany. The opportunity for the Western Allies to capture Berlin and most of eastern Europe was lost and the result was that the Russians took the territory instead.

Various reasons have been given and theories put forward about why Eisenhower gave the order. The official line – supported by Eisenhower and General Omar Bradley – is that the Western Allies were convinced that Berlin was more or less an empty shell and that its capture would be of purely symbolic, rather than military and political, significance.

The 'Alpine Redoubt'

Bradley is clear that Allied commanders were extremely worried about the Germans making their 'last stand' in the 'Alpine Redoubt', a fortress zone in south-west Germany and Austria. Though he gives little detail, Eisenhower also makes the same claim.

Bradley later stated that the Allies had grossly overestimated the extent of German resources in the 'Alpine Redoubt' and feared that any failure to attack that region might lead to considerable strengthening of the Germans' positions there, which would enable them to launch a counter-attack with the deadly weapons of mass destruction that they possessed. It was believed that hundreds of them were stored in underground facilities in the area, including nuclear weapons, and that the 'Alpine Redoubt' would see them launched against the Allies with devastating effect.

There are two schools of thought concerning the 'Alpine Redoubt'. One is that it was a phantom fortress spun out of the vivid imagination of Goebbels. German military intelligence was especially skilful at feeding the Allies with disinformation. As part of the Redoubt myth they issued warnings about the imminent arrival of reinforcements and even placed dummy tanks in the field to deceive photo-reconnaissance planes. Goebbels also made sure that journalists from neutral countries received blood-curdling testimonies to its strength, power and resources.

An alternative view is that the Redoubt existed and was more dangerous than is generally admitted now. Berlin, apart from Hitler and a few senior Nazis in the bunker, had been bombed and shelled into ruins and only a skeleton force of under-equipped troops remained to defend it. By contrast the Thuringian Forest housed the German High Command and many secret military weapons. The aeronautical engineer Sir Roy Fedden, speaking of the Redoubt in 1945, said:

> In these respects, they were not entirely lying. In the course of two recent visits to Germany I have seen enough of their designs and production plans to realize that if they had managed to prolong the war some months longer, we would have been confronted with a set of entirely new and deadly developments in air warfare. There is some reason to believe that Hitler had been promised atomic explosives by October of this year [1945] and if Germany had been first to use them the idea of changing the whole course of the war from a small base in the south-western mountains is by no means so far-fetched.

British intelligence services of the time confirmed Fedden's claims. The reality is that underground airfields and factories were indeed built in the 'Redoubt' area and so were subterranean railways and tunnels to transport weapons. It seems that the most sophisticated and dangerous weapons were transferred to the Redoubt.

The OSS (forerunner of the CIA) also produced intelligence reports declaring that Germany had constructed an 'armed and defended Alpine National Redoubt' from which they planned to 'carry on the fight'. These reports spread alarm among the Allied High Command and Eisenhower, Bradley and Patton began to believe them. After he learned of their existence, Patton wrote gloomily in his diary: 'We can still lose this war.' Eisenhower and Bradley therefore began to believe that capturing Berlin might be less important than closing in on the Redoubt to prevent a last stand by the Germans.

Why did Eisenhower abandon eastern Europe?

Further possible advances by the Western Allies were also prevented. Patton, leading 500,000 men, entered Czechoslovakia with little serious resistance. He was anxious to capture the country ahead of the Soviets and at first Bradley, acting on orders from Eisenhower, gave him full approval to do so. Then, for reasons which remain disputed, Eisenhower rescinded his original order. Patton was ordered not to advance beyond a certain point and to allow the Russian troops to capture the eastern section of the country.

One suggestion is that Stalin bluffed Eisenhower into believing that the Soviet troops were nearer than they actually were. Another is that Eisenhower lost his nerve at the last minute. Others suggest that political considerations – Yalta had assigned Czechoslovakia to the Soviet sphere of influence after the war – made him unwilling to upset the Russians with an independent military action that might be considered hostile. All of these ideas are plausible and all of them might have played a part in Eisenhower's decision.

There are also various conspiracy theories in the field. One is that Eisenhower, in the words of one of his detractors, was 'a conscious agent of the Communist conspiracy'. Others blame Roosevelt or his advisers Bernie Baruch and Harry Hopkins. But to what extent political rather than military considerations guided the decision remains unclear.

The truth will never be known with certainty as many documents from this time remain classified and unavailable even under the Freedom of Information Act. There is no doubt that Eisenhower was extremely 'economical with the truth' in the two books he wrote, where the subject was mentioned briefly, and that Bradley's insistence that faulty intelligence and the overestimation of German strength were responsible is at least partly an excuse rather than a genuine reason for the decision.

Whether the abandonment of eastern Europe to communism was a conscious act of betrayal, a gross military blunder or a mixture of military misjudgement and lack of political will is still open to question. Whatever the reasons for the decision, there is no doubt that its consequences reverberated throughout Europe and the rest of the world for the next 40 years.

WHO PAINTED THE 'NESS GUN BATTERY' MURALS?

A former military installation in the Orkney Islands in Scotland contains an unusual mural. It was painted in World War II and the work is signed by A. R. Woods. Little is known about either the circumstances of the mural or the identity of the artist.

Another painting – this time of Tower Bridge – was sold in an auction in Canada in 2011. It was also signed by A. R. Woods and experts have matched this signature with the one on the Ness Gun Battery mural in the Orkneys. The painting is in a similar style to the Orkney mural. Another painting of the Pool of London is also signed by A. R. Woods and matches the signature and style of the others.

The likeliest candidate for the artist is a former pier master at Tower Pier on the River Thames, Albert John Rycraft Woods, who retired from that position in 1947. He was born at Gravesend in Kent in 1876 and died in 1950.

To confuse the picture, an autobiography by A. P. Woods was published in 1942 entitled *I Guarded the Waterfront*. Its subtitle was *Memoirs of a London Pier Master*. Woods speaks of his time during World War I, saying that:

> *I became a member of the Deptford Battalion, 16th Company, County of London, and before long was made a platoon sergeant. I then went to Albany Street Barracks and there, with the 2nd Life Guards, I underwent a course of training in machine-gunning. I passed out as an instructor.*

The account of his military service only covers World War I, but there is a photograph inside the cover that is exactly the same as the Pool of London painting. Woods also spoke of mounting guns on top of Tower Bridge and firing them at Zeppelin airships attempting to attack London.

No mention is made of any time spent in Orkney and it is curious that A. P. Woods rather than A. R. Woods or A. J. R. Woods is listed as the author of the book. Did the pier master prefer to use a pseudonym for his paintings? Or his autobiography? Or are A. P. Woods and A. R. Woods two different people – in spite of the link between the Pool of London painting and the photograph in his autobiography?

Art critics have remarked that the style of the Ness Gun Battery murals resembles that of a village in Kent. Woods, of course, came from Kent and might have painted the mural while in the Orkneys, to remind him of home.

It seems most likely that A. R. Woods painted all three works and was the pier master at Tower Bridge as well as being the same A. P. Woods whose autobiography was published in 1942. At present the identity of the mystery painter of the Ness Gun mural remains uncertain but that is the most probable explanation of the puzzle.

INDEX

INDEX